REVISED EDITION

THE BIG BOOK ON SMALL GROUPS

JEFFREY ARNOLD

InterVarsity Press
Downers Grove, Illinois

InterVarsity Press
P.O. Box 1400, Downers Grove, IL 60515-1426
World Wide Web: www.ivpress.com
E-mail: mail@ivpress.com

InterVarsity Press® is the book-publishing division of InterVarsity Christian Fellowship/USA®, a student movement active on campus at hundreds of universities, colleges and schools of nursing in the United States of America, and a member movement of the International Fellowship of Evangelical Students. For information about local and regional activities, write Public Relations Dept., InterVarsity Christian Fellowship/USA, 6400 Schroeder Rd., P.O. Box 7895, Madison, WI 53707-7895, or visit the IVCF website at <www.ivcf.org>.

The studies in Appendix A were adapted from Small Group Starter Kit *© 1995 by Jeffrey Arnold.*

Cover design: Cindy Kiple

Cover and interior image: Andrew Craft and Mark Smith

ISBN 0-8308-2370-0

Printed in the United States of America ∞

Library of Congress Cataloging-in-Publication Data

Arnold, Jeffrey.
The big book on small groups / Jeffrey Arnold. — Rev. ed.
p. cm.
ISBN 0-8308-2370-0 (pbk.: alk. paper)
1. Church group work. 2. Small groups — Religious aspects — Christianity. I. Title.
BV652.2.A76 2004
253'.7 — dc22

2003020587

P	20	19	18	17	16	15	14	13	12	11	10	9	8	7	6	5	4	3	2	1
Y	20	19	18	17	16	15	14	13	12	11	10	09	08	07	06	05	04			

To my wife, Karen,

and my children, Brett, Heather and Hannah—

the greatest "small group" in the world!

CONTENTS

INTRODUCTION

I was once invited to speak about small groups in front of a large gathering of pastors from my denomination but, because of an already crowded docket, was given only a few minutes at the end of the meeting to do so. As I pondered my presentation, I settled on a simple yet fairly airtight logic.

I started the presentation by asking, "How many of you have small groups in your churches?" About a third of the pastors raised their hands.

"You might want to reconsider your response to my question," I said. "If you are involved in a congregation, then *every one of you* has small groupings in your congregations. Furthermore, every person in your congregation is in at least one group, and these groups have penetrated absolutely every aspect of the life of your churches. Of course, you may not recognize their presence. If you do, you might call them by their more frequently used name: cliques." From their response, I think they got the point.

Cliques	Small Groups
Closed	Open
Inward-focused	Outward-focused
Controlling Leadership	Spirit-led
Past-oriented	Future-oriented
Elitist	Inclusive
Static	Fluid/Multiplying
Talk	Do
Segmented	Integrated
Unintentional	Intentional

The difference between cliques and small groups

Just think about a church fellowship event. In a large meeting hall full of people, what results? Small groups: clusters of people, usually ranging in size (give or take a few loners) from two to six. The same dynamic tends to hold true for informal gatherings of friends, for committee or service team dynamics, and even (in congregations with predictable worship patterns) for people who sit near each other in sanctuaries, week in and week out. We understand from studying human practices that humans need small groupings for survival, support, emotional strength and stimulation.

WHAT IS THE SMALL GROUP MOVEMENT?

The small group movement, whose roots are in both the early church and later church history, became a broad phenomenon in the late twentieth century. Highly mobile and disconnected people of all ages began to seek deeper fellowship and spiritual nurture in groups. Key leaders began to emerge: Yonggi Cho, Lyman Coleman, Roberta Hestenes and Dawson Trotman, and newer leaders like Bill Donahue, Carl George and Ralph Neighbour. The movement was fueled by key parachurch ministry groups, including InterVarsity Christian Fellowship, Campus Crusade for Christ and the Navigators. Christian publishing houses such as InterVarsity Press and Zondervan began to develop small group curriculum and leader guides, as well as many support materials for leaders. Congregations independent and mainline, charismatic and liturgical, Catholic and Protestant began to embrace groups, and conferences and training events were held all over the world.

What has been the result of such effort and energy? On the positive side, most congregations in the Western world have identifiable groups. Within the broad context of group life, small groups assume a variety of formats, focuses and names. Churches and fellowships offer prayer circles, Bible studies, mission fellowships, sharing and caring groups, evangelistic teams, new member classes, house churches, cell groups, and more.

Even though the groups differ in size and focus, the vast majority possess several common elements. They are small and Christian in orientation, some study occurs, and people feel loved and cared for.

On the other hand, much work remains if this movement is to continue to be vital. Research conducted by academicians, polling firms, publishers, and even secular businesses and institutions has uncovered issues that need to be addressed. Information gained about group dynamics, training and structure issues, and multiplication methods needs to be intentionally taught and modeled if groups are to remain viable and transformative.

For example, although the movement has grown rapidly, many (if not most) groups have become ingrown or focused inward. Why does this matter? First, if churches and ministries are unable to find ways to multiply or create new group opportunities, the vast untouched public will not participate in groups. The movement could die within a matter of generations.

Second, inward-focused groups die. At one time in the small group movement, "family style" life commitments were in vogue in some circles. The idea was that you would make a lifelong commitment to your group, so that the bonds could imitate those of a family. Unfortunately, these long-term groups were nothing like families, because even (especially?) families have an "outward focus." That is, from generation to generation, children are born, move out, find partners, form new families, and so on. A family tree is not a straight line. If it were so, families would die. Inward-focused groups face the same problem.

Another significant concern related to the small group movement is how to touch congregations that have not yet invested in significant group life. Entire books have addressed the subject of bringing renewal to dying Western churches. Yet the inertia, the force that keeps many congregations moving in a slow death pattern, is difficult to overcome.

The current deficits and problems, including the vast number of nonparticipants in life-giving groups, provide a setting for a new generation of leaders to step forward and create new opportunities for group life.

GETTING STARTED

Churches often start small groups without having first addressed the fundamental issues of this ministry:

• How will we form groups?

• Who will lead our groups?

• How do we address problems in groups?

• How will groups relate to our church?

• What happens when a small group becomes a large group?

When leaders are recruited and groups formed without intention, disaster lurks. You have heard the phrase, "Aim at nothing, hit nothing." Actually, the phrase should be restated. "Aim at nothing, hit the wrong thing."

Many individuals and congregations have been damaged by a particular small group or ministry experience. Others have discovered that any positive impact that existed is now past, and they are dealing with an uninvolved congregation, apathetic leaders or members and a ministry that has plateaued or declined.

The Big Book on Small Groups is a training course whose purpose is to introduce new leaders to healthy group principles. Whether you are starting a ministry from nothing, attempting to revitalize an existing ministry or training leaders for a vital ministry, this resource offers help with the most fundamental issue that every church or fellowship must answer: how to train leaders.

The Big Book on Small Groups was first published in 1991. This updated version includes new material, fresh insight and improvements suggested by those who used the original book.

The course can be used by a variety of group types within a range of group structures. Leaders of cell groups, care groups, nurture groups, committees, ministry teams, Bible studies and healing groups will find the material useful and adaptable.

The first four chapters are designed to be the core small-group training course, while the remaining eight chapters can be used for follow-up training. Of course, the material can also be implemented within an intentional twelve-week training program.

This training material is easily adaptable for an individual learning alone, a one-on-one setting (coach-leader or leader-apprentice), a small group of potential leaders (also called a "turbo" group, since every trained leader may form a group), or a Sunday school environment. It can be crafted for use in weekend training, four-week training (with monthly follow-up meetings in which chapters five through twelve are discussed) and twelve-week training formats.

For coaches and trainers, material in the appendixes will guide you in how to better use this resource. At the end of each chapter you will find a section titled "Ideas for Coaches/Trainers." There you'll find helpful exercises and discussion points as you walk leaders through the training process.

GROUP PHILOSOPHY

This material will work best when used in conjunction with your own church's small group materials. These materials need to address strategic issues such as how people are placed in groups, what the leadership support structure looks like, and what types and names of groups are used in your particular setting. To help you ask and answer these key questions, I refer you to another book I wrote, *Starting Small Groups: Creating Communities That Matter* (Abingdon Press).

When *The Big Book on Small Groups* was first published, there were few significant small group resources. In the 1990s, however, many key books were published, including some that have deeply changed the way group life is perceived in the local congregation.

The simplest small group model is the "cell church," proposed by church leaders Ralph Neighbour (*Where Do We Go From Here?* [Touch Publications]) and Joel Comiskey. A cell church, in general, is a congregation that uses two key ministry elements: worship (celebration) and small groups (also called multiplying cells). Cell churches tend to dispense with "program" and age-oriented ministries, choosing instead to perform the key church ministries (care, counsel, nurture, support and worship, and ministry to adults, children, youth and so on) in cell groups. These groups are led by lay leaders, and when groups grow, they multiply. Once a week (or, depending on the congregation, perhaps once a month) the cells then gather for a celebration—a worship service.

A second model, proposed by Carl George (*Prepare Your Church for the Future* [Revell Publishing]), is the "meta" model. It possesses similar traits to the cell model, including multiplying groups and the corporate worship and celebration of these groups. But the meta model incorporates a third, perhaps more "traditional" element of church life called "congregation." This layer of church life recognizes more program-oriented elements such as Sunday school classes, training events and age-appropriate outreach events. Instead of perceiving those ministries as ends to themselves, however, the meta model views them as gathering events ("fishing ponds") that can draw people into group life.

A third model, which modifies George's meta approach, embraces the idea of "a church of small groups" (Bill Donahue, *Building A Church of Small Groups* [Zondervan]). This model recognizes both the importance of connected, accountable, multiplying groups *and* important aspects of congregational life that, while not "small group" experiences in a technical sense, benefit from group principles.

A FINAL WORD

Whether you are an experienced facilitator of groups, an apprentice or a first-time leader, welcome! You are about to enter an experience designed to train you to make disciples for Jesus Christ in community. My desire in preparing this book is that as the gospel is preached and disciples begin to follow Jesus, he will receive the honor and obedience that are due him, and his kingdom will be extended to the ends of the earth. Small groups play a vital part in that process, so let's get started!

1

THE POWER
OF SMALL GROUPS

Rob and Jenny wandered into Second Church because they felt like they were missing something from life. They had met in college, lived together in the years following, and eventually gotten married. A child, Ian, soon followed.

If they had been able to articulate the spiritual search that took them to Second Church, they probably would have said that they were hoping the church would fill a void in their lives. They were unaware of the possibilities that Jesus Christ offers and of the presence of the Spirit of God, who was drawing them into God's community of faith.

Rob and Jenny may have been ambiguous about the notion of spiritual journey, but Second Church was not. Second Church was very intentional about drawing people into a relationship with Christ, and into small discipleship groups where they could be cared for and nurtured.

Rob and Jenny were invited to a church picnic, and at the picnic a member of the church spoke to them about the group he led. When

Rob and Jenny indicated interest in the group, the group welcomed them.

Participating in a healthy group whose members openly sought God's direction was both puzzling and invigorating to Rob and Jenny. They asked lots of questions. The group patiently loved them and answered their questions. Ironically, Rob and Jenny's desire to learn renewed the group and deepened its commitment. At the same time, the group's love and the prodding of the Spirit brought Rob and Jenny gently into the kingdom of God.

That was just the beginning. Rob and Jenny were part of the group when Terri was invited, and they were instrumental in strengthening her faith while she went through a painful divorce. Later, they were apprentice leaders when two baby-Christian couples began to attend. Within a few years they led a group when the group they were in multiplied.

All this occurred because a caring person at a picnic was prepared to invite them to participate in an authentic Christian community.

JESUS' METHOD OF MAKING DISCIPLES

Jesus Christ is our first and greatest model for how small groups can stimulate faith and growth in others. In Jesus' first-century world, disciples were usually the students of a particular teacher, apprentices who learned all that their master could teach so they could go on to become masters themselves. In addition to teaching the Jewish law and the traditions of Moses, the teachers (or rabbis) sought to train their disciples to live out their faith as obedient followers of God. In Christ's call to discipleship, he challenged the disciples to be with him, to learn his ways and, going beyond the parameters of other rabbis, to proclaim the good news of his kingdom to others.

Being with him. The call "Follow me" had a very real application.

Jesus did not say these words and then walk away, never to be seen by the disciples again. He expected them to leave what they were doing to physically walk after him.

For three years after this call, the twelve disciples lived with him. They traveled to many different places, and sought food and shelter in a host of ways. They saw Jesus in the morning when he got up and at night when he lay down. They watched him pray, heal, preach and teach. They observed Jesus in his dealings with difficult people. Through all of their experiences with him, they learned that Jesus' lifestyle was radically different from the one they had learned from birth. They were challenged to a new life.

Learning his ways. This new life did not come easily to them. The disciples were naturally brash, selfish and uncaring. Jesus had to teach them to be courageous, gentle, giving and compassionate. On many occasions he took the disciples aside (for example, the Sermon on the Mount) to instruct them. When he told parables, he would explain the meaning to them after the crowds had departed. Indeed, the disciples were often as dense as the crowds when it came to understanding the parables! He asked questions of them, taught them, admonished them, prodded them to take steps of faith, nurtured them and loved them.

Theirs was a special relationship that, for two reasons, went deeper than what Jesus had with the crowds that followed him. First, Jesus committed himself to the disciples in every way. He made himself accessible to them and confided in them, calling them his friends. Because he committed himself to his disciples, Jesus had great expectations of them.

Second, in return, the disciples were committed to Jesus. Since Jesus supplied the brains and purpose for the fledgling Christian movement, the disciples were not able to add much to the process. What they did bring was a growing love for Christ and an awakening desire to be obedient and loyal in everything. They struggled with their faith, sin and weaknesses, but they wanted to be faithful. They loved Jesus and became willing to give up everything (eventually, most of them even gave their lives) for this man from Galilee.

Proclaiming the good news to others. One of the marks of good students is that they are able to do what the teacher has instructed them to do—even when the teacher is not present. As the disciples traveled with Jesus, they were able to do some helpful things, but they spent most of their time observing the master at work. Then, Jesus sent them out two by two to prepare towns for his coming. They preached as they had seen Jesus preach. They sought faithful, God-fearing people in the towns as Jesus had done. They healed the sick and comforted the bereaved. And they learned what ministry was all about. In being sent out from Jesus, they learned even more about how to imitate their rabbi.

We examine Jesus' means of making disciples because the Master's way of molding lives is still superior to any other model we could imitate. We see in the Gospels that living as Christ's disciple is complicated. Many lessons must be learned. What did it take for Christ to make a powerful difference through his followers? Nothing other than a personal investment in their lives.

THE EARLY CHURCH AND DISCIPLE-MAKING

After Jesus returned to the Father, his disciples began to duplicate his kind of ministry. In the book of Acts much can be discovered about the history of the church of Christ. Following Christ's ascension into heaven, the promised Holy Spirit empowered the disciples to start carrying the good news to all people.

It was an exciting time for the church, a period of rapid growth in spite of tremendous persecution. Peter's sermon in Acts 2 brought three thousand new believers into the church in one day! These new believers joined with other disciples to worship in the temple each day. Just imagine the uproar their meetings must have caused in the already crowded temple courtyard! Yet their lives were so different that they were viewed favorably by others, and the church grew daily.

Initially, the church met together in larger groups and at the temple or in synagogues for corporate worship. But small groups also had a place in the life of the church after Pentecost and an even more significant role in later years, as persecution drove the church underground.

The apostles and early church teachers and elders went from house to house, visiting small groups in homes as they taught and made disciples (Acts 5:42). People met together in their homes to break bread together and to use the opportunity to encourage each other to live out their faith in ever greater obedience. There were home prayer meetings like the one held while Peter was in prison (Acts 12:12), and Paul's letters allude to "house churches" (Romans 16:5).

Whether house churches were independent groups of believers or were parts of larger churches is uncertain. It is likely, however, that small house fellowships were the building blocks of the church in each city or region. The early disciples met in groups small enough to fit into normal homes. (Note that Priscilla and Aquila were tentmakers and probably not wealthy. See Acts 18:3.)

The church needed the house church for its survival. There were periods of intense persecution for the first few centuries after Christ, so the early church was often not able to meet openly, nor were they allowed to purchase large buildings for gathering. They relied on the more protective environment of the home to nurture and protect the gospel in the lives of believers. Somehow the church was able to multiply without large buildings, mass meetings and a plethora of "how to" books.

SMALL GROUPS IN TODAY'S CHURCH

Small group experts and theologians have noted many other biblical arguments for small groups. They have observed that in the creation and fall narratives of Genesis 1—3, human beings are depicted in relationship with God and dependent on one another. They have seen small group principles and ideals in the Jewish social structure, the law of God and the *one anothers* of the New Testament. (See, for instance, Gareth Icenogle's *Biblical Foundations for Small Group Ministry* [InterVarsity Press].)

But are these principles, ideals and practices still relevant today? A person might be tempted to think, *That was then; this is now.* Small groups might work in a measured, agrarian culture, but do they have a place in fast-paced, modern world?

A fascinating aspect of discipleship is that Christians in the twenty-first century are in a direct line that can be traced back to the original twelve disciples. In 2 Timothy 2:2, Paul illustrates the process of disciple-making in the following way: "And the things you have heard me say in the presence of many witnesses entrust to reliable men who will also be qualified to teach others." Thus, all disciples of Christ have been entrusted with the gospel message, which they are to continually invest in the lives of others. Rather than ending with us, the process must begin anew with us, as with each new generation.

The key strategic question for individuals and congregations isn't *Do we have small groups in our church?* That should be obvious. Here are the real questions we should be asking ourselves about our small groupings (friendship clusters, work teams and so on):

- Are we introducing Christian disciplines into our small groupings?

- Are our small groupings building the kingdom or hindering the kingdom?

- Are we training leaders who bring Christian disciplines into small groupings?

- Is our entire congregation working to develop a disciplined small group mentality?

In this book we are focusing on reversing the key attributes that make cliques unhealthy, so that we are not trapped by the inward, unfocused and random nature of the undisciplined groupings scattered throughout our congregations and fellowships. If we do not focus on returning to our biblical roots by building intentional community, we will miss the greatest lessons that our faith offers.

As we observed with Jesus, disciples are best made in community. Unlike cliques, however, these communities or groupings are intentionally small, outward in focus and intent on participating with Christ in the building of his kingdom. Here is a working definition of a Christ-centered small group:

> A small group is intent on participating with Christ in building
> his ever-expanding kingdom in the hearts of individuals, in the
> life of the group and, through believers, into the world.

DISCIPLE-MAKING THROUGH GROUPS

Disciples are made intentionally. Just as children don't grow up without personal care, or learn mathematics on their own, so discipleship will not occur without faithful Christians being intentional about meeting together. The word *discipleship* is a catch phrase in the church today, often without meaning. As a result, some people think of discipleship when they think of Bible study workbooks or adult Sunday school. What they forget is that the process of disciple-making is a dynamic relationship between fellow Christians and their Lord, and that it is marked by continued progress.

You cannot pay lip service to disciple-making or look at it as one aspect of ministry. It must be the goal of all ministry, that people will come to faith and then grow to maturity as Christ's disciples. This first principle will become a reality in your church or fellowship if even just a few people take seriously Christ's command to make disciples and start acting on that basis.

Disciples are to be like Christ. Have you ever noticed people, perhaps children, who are devoted to a particular celebrity, and who dress, talk and walk like the individual they idolize? It is only natural to emulate someone you respect and look up to. Imitating Christ is not the end of discipleship, however. New Testament writers, most notably Paul, speak of a far higher goal: *that Christ may be formed in us.* In small groups and with other believers, we "practice" the Christian life together in community; then, Scripture teaches us, the Spirit of God works to apply lessons learned into the deepest recesses of our hearts. We become, in the deepest sense, like Christ.

Modern Christians may have difficulty perceiving themselves as disciples. We ask people if they are Christians instead of if they are disciples, as if you could be a Christian without being a disciple. In the early church, followers of Christ were called disciples until someone in Antioch thought of the term *Christian* (Acts 11:26). There is nothing wrong with using the word *Christian* as it is properly understood: *Christian* means "belonging to Christ."

Disciples are made in relationship. As you think back over your life, you can no doubt think of many things that you learned by watching and then imitating. This is how we learn to ride a bike, drive a car and lift weights. It is also how we learn to "act cool" in high school, move up the social ladder in adulthood and age gracefully in older years. We learn about life through the relationships in which we participate.

The Christian life is the same. There is no example in the Scriptures of a lone disciple. Even Paul, after his dramatic conversion and a long stay in the desert, went to Jerusalem and associated himself with the apostles and later with the church at Antioch (Acts 9:26-30; 11:25). When he planted churches, he always traveled in the company of others. At different times he formed a team relationship with Barnabas, Silas and Timothy, among others. The relational, community-based model of disciple-making had been demonstrated by Jesus and the disciples, and it provided the necessary support for Paul and the early church in the turbulent period after Pentecost.

Since we learn best in relationship, we most effectively learn to be disciples that way. But disciples produced through loving community in modern churches are too rare. The self-sufficient individualism of Western culture has seeped into the church and led to situations in which individuals are trying, often without notable success, to mature alone in their faith. Many resources—Christian books, videos, conferences, tape series—are available for these lone disciples to increase their knowledge about Jesus. But an accumulation of facts and ideas is only the beginning. We need a community of fellow disciples who can help us learn to live a life transformed by the Holy Spirit. In fact, *growing in community* is such an important concept that it provides the basis for the names given to most of my chapters ("A Studying Community," and so forth). Without a community in which we can learn, practice, fail and eventually move out as agents of change, we are left without a secure foundation.

THE COMMUNITY OF FAITH

I opened this chapter with a story about several people whose lives were touched through a small group. What we cannot miss from stories like that is how God then uses those people to bless others. If

you possess faith in Christ and have a clear focus and positive training, you may engage in face-to-face Christian community with others. Soon other people hungering for real community will follow. In
the next chapter, we will examine what church body life is all about,
and why people need it.

QUESTIONS FOR REVIEW

1. Who (or what) has been an important influence in your own spiritual life, to lead you to Christ or to help you grow in your faith?

2. Based on what you read in this chapter, what are some of the
   practical results of Jesus' disciple-making?

3. How were small groups used to build the early church?

4. What are key differences between a healthy group and a clique?

5. Explain each of these statements:
   a. Disciples are made intentionally.
   b. Disciples are to be like Christ.
   c. Disciples are made in relationship.

READING FOR REFLECTION

For a more thorough biblical and theological overview of groups,
see Gareth Icenogle's *Biblical Foundations for Small Groups* (Inter-
Varsity Press).

    For thorough analyses of the cell and meta models of small groups,
see *Prepare Your Church for the Future* by Carl George (Revell Publishing) and *Where Do We Go From Here?* by Ralph Neighbour
(Touch Publications).

    A wonderful resource that also explores groups' connection to the
church is *Building a Church of Small Groups* by Bill Donahue and
Russ Robinson (Zondervan).

IDEAS FOR COACHES/TRAINERS

The material in this book, along with the suggested activities, is best used at least part of the time in groups of three to four people. Therefore, if you are training a larger group, provide time for small group interaction.

The best training for small group leaders is to be in a small group. If the participants in a training course are not in a small group or have not been in a small group, locate some kind of small group study and use part of the training time for people to simply participate in a small group.

Make sure you take time for chapter review and questions about the chapter each week.

For larger training events, in the first session(s) take time for people to get to know each other.

SESSION 1 IDEAS

- Exercise: A friend of yours from another congregation is talking to you about how your church uses small groups. She says, "Well, that's great how you use groups. But our church is small, and we are like a family. We don't need groups." Prepare a response for your friend based on biblical, theological and ecclesiastical grounds.

- Strategy: The first session provides a key opportunity for you to introduce the learners to your own church's material on small groups. In this first session, you may choose to pass out any material you have and provide a brief overview, perhaps assigning reading for the coming meetings. In subsequent sessions you will be prompted to explain parts of your strategy and goals.

2

BUILDING THE CHURCH THROUGH SMALL GROUPS

Have you ever seen the inside of a beehive? If so, then you have had the opportunity to observe thousands of tiny creatures working feverishly, going in countless directions. Some leave the hive to locate and bring back nectar (used to produce honey) and pollen (to feed the young). Another crew works in the honey section to fill and cap honey. Still another works with the "brood" (the eggs), nurturing them until they are born. A smaller group attaches to the queen bee to protect her.

The beehive is a good illustration of how individuals can work together for one common goal. There is very little time to bicker when each bee's contribution is necessary for survival. When each different group makes its contribution, the hive is strong.

Similarly, body life assumes the bringing together of unique Christians working for a common goal—to be and make disciples. The ideal group engages each member in discipleship while encouraging each individual to make a positive contribution for the growth of others.

Imagine asking a group of church members to brainstorm a list of qualities that they would desire for their pastor. "Just spend a few moments dreaming about the ideal pastor," you might ask. What qualities would you love for this person to possess? These qualities can relate to personality, style, character, spirituality, maturity, relationships and more.

After the group brainstorms and refines its lists, imagine combining the different lists on white-board and weeding out qualities that are redundant or unreasonable. We could assume at least a couple of hundred legitimate qualities placed on the board:

- loves children

- is accessible

- has a great family

- knows Scripture

- is a good administrator and people manager

- and so on

Once the list is compiled, ask if anybody present either possesses all of those qualities or knows someone with all of those qualities. The answer would have to be no. Well, perhaps most of the qualities? Again, no.

One wonders, then, how all of these legitimate expectations can be met. Who is able to relate to all ages, completely fulfill the various functions of the church, live a balanced life and train people to live victorious lives?

When that question is posed, most participants might first respond, "Well, we're looking for Jesus, aren't we?" Perhaps. But instead of asking what we would like in a pastor, we could be asking, "Where can we find every desired quality that we have placed on the board?"

The answer is the church—the body of Christ.

THE WAY THE BODY WORKS

Consider a congregation with no more than fifty members and participants from the perspective of our ideal-qualities-in-a-pastor scenario. Logic suggests that within that body will be people gifted (with spiritual gifts) and skilled for every possible need. We can assume, for example, that at least one person will have the gifts of compassion and mercy, and will be able to visit shut-ins and those who are sick (functions, incidentally, which are automatically assigned to pastors in most congregations or parishes). Think we can find a prayer warrior? A servant? Someone with carpentry skills? Most likely. In summary, the body of Christ includes the full list of character qualities, the sum total of what we want in a pastor. The key strategic question becomes, How can we enable each of our people to be a fully functioning Christian, serving the body and kingdom of Christ?

Perhaps every Christian would agree that every Christian should serve and that the ideal church functions like a body, with every part working for the common good. Yet in the Western world, congregations struggle to engage people in ministry and service. Many congregations experience the 20/80 rule, with 20 percent of their members serving and the other 80 percent taking passive roles.

Why is this so? There are many reasons, including a consumer mentality among church members with a constant need for feeding and a desire for ease and simplicity. But one possible solution to this problem is to examine the nature and character of the church, and to define the essential activities of a gathered body of Christ in whatever expression.

Ephesians 4:11-16 uses imagery from the human body to depict an alive fellowship of believers.

> It was he who gave some to be apostles, some to be prophets, some to be evangelists, and some to be pastors and teachers, to prepare God's people for works of service, so that the body of

Christ may be built up until we all reach unity in the faith and in the knowledge of the Son of God and become mature, attaining to the whole measure of the fullness of Christ. Then we will no longer be infants, tossed back and forth by the waves, and blown here and there by every wind of teaching and by the cunning and craftiness of men in their deceitful scheming. Instead, speaking the truth in love, we will in all things grow up into him who is the Head, that is, Christ, From him the whole body, joined and held together by every supporting ligament, grows and builds itself up in love, as each part does its work.

In this passage and others like it, Christ functions as the head. Every activity of the body should be initiated by him, and the result of every activity should flow back to him. Each Christian is a part of the body. As members of the body, we are reliant on one another and on Christ, and mutually responsible to use whatever contribution we make to grow the body into maturity.

WHAT KIND OF SMALL GROUPS?

So how does the church create specific opportunities for the body of Christ to achieve the kind of maturity spoken of in Ephesians, while engaging in the activities that build the church? Small groups.

Your church may be so large that individuals who need accountability to grow are getting lost in the crowd. Or it may be so small that a surface familiarity defines relationships. Perhaps some of the members of your church are looking for an opportunity to develop a Christ-centered lifestyle in partnership with others who feel the same calling.

In healthy groups, as friendship deepens, members are able to challenge one another to take new steps in growth. Growing Christians find new reasons to worship and thank God together. Out of this kind of community comes a sense of joyful challenge that draws others to join them as they seek opportunities for growth. The possibilities are limitless.

We must be careful, however, to differentiate between healthy small groups and unhealthy ones. Not all small groups provide a positive impact. If structured carelessly, small groups can hinder growth, exclude people, provide platforms for negative or destructive personalities, and keep people from reaching their potential for service and outreach.

Therefore, we must focus on building groups *with certain qualities.* Those qualities can be derived from Jesus' practice and from Scripture, and are located in our working definition of small groups: A *small group is intent on participating with Christ in building his ever-expanding kingdom in the hearts of individuals, in the life of the group and, through believers, into the world.*

This definition seeks to locate Christ's transformative, kingdom-building activity within the three different relationships reflected in Ephesians: the individual's relationship with the group (the inward dimension); Christ's relationship with the individual and group (the upward dimension); and the individual's and group's witness to the world (the outward dimension).

Whenever churches or groups are in a state of growth and renewal, it is not because they are developing one area of body life (for example, building a strong relationship with Christ) to the exclusion of the others (group care and outreach). Strong churches/groups/movements, whether schooled in Scripture or church history, are healthy precisely because they do in a holistic manner what the church (body) does when it gathers. The next chapter looks into the specific activities of groups when they gather. For the rest of this chapter, we will examine the positive benefits that come from obediently participating in this three-dimensional, holistic group life.

GROUPS REACHING INWARD (GROUP CARE)

Groups provide love and care for their members in many ways. A loving community offers members a positive body life experience by engaging people in the discovery of their spiritual gifts, developing the lay leadership of a church, and caring for its members.

Discovering spiritual gifts. Imagine someone like Christina, a relatively new believer in the process of becoming involved in a local church. To Christina, the Sunday morning service seemed so well planned and the praise team so well rehearsed that, although she loved to attend, there really did not seem to be anything she could offer. There were plenty of activities in the church — suppers, work days and retreats among them — but someone else always seemed to be supplying the leadership and gifts necessary for those functions. Of course there were needs in the nursery and with Vacation Bible School, but Christina knew she was not very good at working with children.

Then Christina joined a small group that met in Bill and Sue's home. One week Sue asked Christina if she would coordinate refreshments for the next month. Christina agreed, and in the process she discovered a new and better way for the group to share responsibility for refreshments, cleanup and childcare. One night Bill asked Christina to plan the group's upcoming workday at the community soup kitchen. She demonstrated a great deal of sensitivity when bringing together the small group members and the soup kitchen staff, and the day was a success.

When the small group decided they would like to have a weekend retreat together, Christina volunteered to organize it. She collected ideas from the members, delegated responsibilities and worked out the many logistical details. Everyone agreed that the retreat was wonderful. By then Bill and Sue realized that Christina had the gift of administration. They mentioned it to the church's central planning group, and the next time the church began planning a major project, Christina was asked to take responsibility for it.

Everyone benefited from the discovery of Christina's gift. She was able to develop her gift of administration in the midst of a loving community where she was affirmed and encouraged to use her gift to serve others. Bill and Sue had the satisfaction of helping Christina mature and start using her gift. The church leaders had another resource person for projects. And those in the church who were exhausted from always being called on to do things were stimulated by her enthusiasm and help.

This story can be retold with respect to any number of gifts for ministry that are desperately needed in churches today—leading worship, teaching, giving money, showing mercy, doing evangelism and so on. (See Rom 12:4-8; 1 Cor 12:4-11.) The bottom line is that individuals are often hesitant to explore their spiritual gifts in a large group. Sometimes they are willing to serve but are overlooked in the crowd. Or perhaps they have been "plugged" into church ministries where they do not fit. Healthy, intentional small groups allow people to stimulate each other and, as a result, to put their God-given gifts to use for building the church.

Developing lay leadership. Imagine what it was like when Bill and Sue came to our hypothetical church five years ago. They met the pastor and a number of new people at the regular Sunday activities, but it took a long time to get to know people beyond a surface level. The pastor and church members liked Bill and Sue but didn't really know much about them.

Eventually Bill and Sue joined a small group led by Steve. Steve soon realized that Bill and Sue were mature disciples who possessed leadership ability. He asked them if they would be interested in "apprenticing" with him, or learning how to lead groups (more in chapters four and eleven). They prayed about it and agreed, so for the next few months Bill and Sue helped Steve with various leadership tasks within the group. They also participated in their church's small group leader training classes.

Then, when Steve's group was ready to multiply, Bill and Sue were prepared to lead. They became small group leaders, and as they became more visible within the church they were occasionally asked to take on other leadership roles that fit their gifts.

The pastor and other church leaders might never have recognized Bill and Sue's potential as lay leaders if there had not been an opportunity to know them better and observe them interacting with other people. Small groups provide that opportunity. They can be the key to finding "anonymous" members, discovering their leadership potential and developing that potential for the benefit of the church. In this way the church finds that the ministry of the many replaces the ministry of the few.

Practicing effective congregational care. Imagine another member of Bill and Sue's group. Eugene's wife died several years ago, but to all appearances he had been getting along very well on his own. He had a good job and could take care of the house and fix his own meals. In church services he appeared to be happy and at peace.

In the privacy of his home, however, he often felt very lonely. He became depressed on Sundays as he watched families leaving church together. He longed to have his family intact again. Unfortunately, his children and grandchildren lived too far away to visit on weekends.

One night while everyone was having coffee and dessert after a small group meeting, Sue asked Eugene how things were going for him. Since he knew Sue and trusted her, and since she had taken the trouble to ask, Eugene shared his feelings of loneliness. Several other group members overheard the conversation and joined in, showing deep care for Eugene. As a result, the group members took turns inviting him to spend Sunday afternoons with their families.

Deeply personal needs like Eugene's often go unrecognized in a church. People like Eugene are not likely to voice their needs without being asked. Even if someone does care enough to ask, who can meet the need? Bill and Sue were able to call on others in their group so that no one person or family felt overburdened.

We could offer numerous scenarios that demonstrate how small groups can care. Groups can provide tangible support (cars, babysitting, meals), intangible support (love, comfort, care) and prayer support. They can also be used in the larger church through outreach, visitation and other forms of service. Groups can also stand by people in situations involving prolonged illness, chronic conditions (such as certain forms of depression) and long-term trials (such as extended unemployment). Small groups, with their grassroots relationships, can contribute to the health of the body by loving those in need.

GROUPS REACHING UPWARD (NURTURE AND WORSHIP)

Small groups are a great means of helping a congregation to care deeply for fellowship members. We are not, however, to be in the business of teaching people to be nice to one another. What makes a small group experience truly transforming is learning and applying biblical truth. This is why groups that meet regularly engage in nurture and worship.

Nurture. When Bill and Sue started the group, they knew that the first few weeks of group life would involve focusing on helping group members get to know one another. Ultimately, however, their vision for group life involved connecting people to God as revealed in Scripture.

In the fall, just several weeks after the group started, they worked through a six-week Bible study on the book of Philippians. The study whetted the group's appetite for more and deeper knowledge. When Christina returned from vacation enthused about a book she had read, the group decided to study the book together. When the book study was completed, the group (after praying) decided to engage in a Bible study that involved homework.

Over time, Bill and Sue's group was able to benefit from the study of Bible books and helpful Christian resources. Group members discovered that their knowledge of God's Word and their confidence in his promises and trustworthiness increased with every passing month.

Thanksgiving and praise. Bill, Sue, Christina, Eugene and other members of the group had been praying for the healing of one of their members, Michelle. Michelle recovered, and they all rejoiced in God's grace. When Kevin was looking for a job, they prayed, and he was able to locate employment. Once again, the group gave thanks. In the process, they discovered that God was listening, ready and able to answer their prayers. Many times their prayers were answered in a manner that they had not anticipated, opening new avenues of discovery about the nature and character of God.

There were other ways that the group was able to worship. As they experienced the depth of community, they felt God's love. When they confessed sin together, they were able to experience God's mercy. When they took time to sing, they felt his presence. Little by little, they learned a lifestyle of responding to God.

When enough people in a congregation start experiencing these worship moments, the entire church begins to change. Spiritual renewal that begins in groups can begin to create revival in the larger body of Christ.

GROUPS REACHING OUTWARD (SERVICE AND EVANGELISM)

One of the inherent weaknesses in any small grouping of people is the natural tendency to maintain an inward focus (care), ignoring the outward focus (service and evangelism). This tendency is literally as old as sin, since because of sin humans are prone to self-centeredness and self-preservation. We can reasonably assume, therefore, that an outward focus is the most difficult of the group disciplines to cultivate. It is, however, an indispensable trait of healthy groups. Because of the powerful dynamics that accompany small group outreach, an outward focus can keep a group vital, refreshed and challenged.

Evangelism. If people like Bill and Sue had difficulty discovering their niche in the church, you can guess how much harder it was for someone like Carolyn, who did not yet know Christ. Drawn by the Holy Spirit toward Christ, she needed a venue that would allow her to ask questions and seek answers. But she was intimidated walking into a church full of strangers, so Sue invited her into the small group. For Carolyn the small group was crucial in establishing her relationship with Christ and a new church.

What about people who would be unlikely to go near a church building on their own? Christina had a friend at work named David, with whom she was eager to share Christ's love. David had refused to consider attending worship with her, but when Christina told him about her friends in a small group, he was willing to visit. The group welcomed him and eventually led him to discuss faith in Christ. He became a Christian and later joined the church. This happened because God used the small group to meet David at a point where he felt somewhat comfortable—a home, with friends. His resistance to Christ and the church was broken down in a loving environment.

Biblical evangelism is not a program but a person-to-person process of sharing the good news about forgiveness of sin and new life in Jesus. Because small groups are likely to be the most personal setting offered by a church, they are natural places for this kind of evangelism to take place. In addition, groups provide a rallying point for evangelism opportunities (more in chapter eleven).

Spiritual and numerical growth. Many frustrated pastors have tried program after program to resurrect lethargic congregations, often focusing on one particular aspect of the Christian life (such as prayer) at a time, as if one area can be dealt with apart from others. Small groups provide a format where every area of the Christian life can be experienced in a loving community.

Small groups attract and keep new church members like David. Seekers like Carolyn find a caring group to support them as they grow. Mature disciples like Bill and Sue are able to exercise leadership because of groups. In these ways and many more, small groups provide a place to sink roots and grow for people who might otherwise end up on the margins of a church.

What would happen if more than one third of your church's members participated in healthy, growing groups? Would your church be different than a church with no groups? Absolutely! Healthy groups will attach people deeply to their God and show them how to minister to the world.

Multiplication. The development of growth models for small group ministry, including the meta and cell models, reflects a concern among pastors and small group leaders about multiplication—the experience of a healthy group becoming two groups. In a perfect world, multiplication progresses as these two groups eventually give birth to more groups, and the process continues as more persons come to commit their lives to Christ. Multiplication is a powerful way to influence the world for Christ.

CONCLUSION

We've seen some of the benefits and possibilities that healthy groups offer to individuals, groups, congregations and communities. In order to experience those benefits, the first key building block of the small group ministry is the trained leader. The next chapter explores how effective leaders can guide groups and individuals into a deep practice and experience of the inward, upward and outward life of the church.

QUESTIONS FOR REVIEW

1. What are the three most significant qualities you would look for in a pastor?

2. Based on the first part of the chapter, where can you find the gifts and skills needed to construct a healthy church?

3. In what ways are many congregations today *not* like the body of Christ as depicted in Scripture?

4. What are three activities or relationships of a healthy, holistic small group?

5. How would the absence of a developed inward life (group care) be harmful to a group?

6. How would the absence of a developed upward life (nurture and worship) be harmful to a group?

7. How would the absence of a developed outward life (service and evangelism) be harmful to a group?

8. Of all of the positive benefits groups can bring to a church, which to you are most compelling?

9. What are several ways your church or fellowship could benefit from healthy groups?

READING FOR REFLECTION

For an analysis of the strengths and weaknesses of the small group movement, see Robert Wuthnow's *Sharing the Journey: Support Groups and America's New Quest for Community* (Free Press).

For resources that reflect on biblical community, see *Jesus and Community* by Gerard Lohfink (Fortress); *A Peculiar People* by Rodney Clapp (InterVarsity Press); and *Theology for the Community of God* by Stanley Grenz (Broadman and Holman).

IDEAS FOR COACHES/TRAINERS

- Write a skit or worship commercial that you may (or may not) use for your congregation, in which you expound on one key benefit that groups bring to the congregation.

- Have people in small group leadership training fill a paper bag with various small items. Then have them write a skit using (1) one benefit of small groups and (2) everything in the bag.

- Look over your own church's strategy (if you have one) with participants in your training program. Focus on how small groups are connected to your church.

3

BECOMING A LEADER

You have been hiking for five miles with a fifty-pound pack on your back as part of a weekend wilderness adventure with a group of other business people, in the hope of relieving some of the stress and strain of everyday living. The day is clear, the air is crisp, and you hope to get some beautiful panoramic shots with your camera.

The group has had a hard time getting started. No one knew how to pack the backpacks, so many things have clattered noisily during the hike. Some of the smaller members of the group are having an especially hard time with their packs, and one person is limping badly from a fall he took a few miles back. As you struggle with your own pack, you wonder when the group leader will call for a break.

The leader doesn't seem to have noticed that there are problems. You can see him hopping merrily in front of the group—probably because he doesn't have a pack of his own. When asked why he didn't have a pack, he told the group that the experience was theirs, not his. He needed to be free to stay in front and point the way for the group.

Eventually the group comes to a cliff, and the leader consults his map. Sure enough, this looks like the cliff he is going to teach you to rappel on. You lower your pack to the ground while the leader gives instructions and gathers the rappelling supplies. You are nervous as you prepare to receive your training. Ladders scare you enough—how much more the sheer wall of a cliff? An encouraging thought, however, is that a number of your friends have rappeled and lived through it. They had taken lessons from expert mountain climbers and had felt a great sense of accomplishment.

The leader hooks the belt around the first rappeler. As you move closer to the edge, you can see the climber's face. She looks pale and afraid. But the leader, who appears undaunted by her response, is giving instructions in a firm, clear voice. As he continues on, however, concern appears on the faces of the other group hikers. He isn't making sense.

One group member timidly raises her hand and asks him how many times he has rappeled. As he urges the nervous first rappeler toward the edge he says, "Why, I've never rappeled before in my life! I'm scared to death of heights. But don't worry, I'm sure I'm doing this the right way. I've watched this being done two or three times . . . "

WALKING YOUR TALK

Would you trust your life to a rappelling instructor who didn't know what he was talking about? Most likely not. We rightly stay away from rappelling instructors who have never been on the face of a cliff. Until they have lived through the experience themselves, they cannot identify with the struggles, fears and real dangers that come from rappelling.

The "leader" in this hiking story did not carry a pack, was not sensitive to the needs of others and was not qualified to lead the group in rappelling. He was not a leader at all. A rappelling teacher needs to feel what it is like to dangle from the face of a cliff. In the same way, the Christian leader needs to understand the struggles and challenges facing an active Christian lifestyle.

Sometimes those of us who live in democratic societies are uncomfortable with the idea of leadership. We feel the necessity to affirm the worth of every individual, so we are hesitant to single out any one person as somehow "better" than the rest. But effective Christian leaders are not of greater value than others. Instead, they are experienced servants who seek to build up the body of Christ. They are people in whom others recognize maturity and a desire for continued growth. They are willing to offer whatever spiritual gifts they possess to serve their churches.

Many people are standing at the "cliff edge" of Christian discipleship, just waiting for someone to lead them. With the proper supervision, they will discover new perspectives and dimensions in life. When they reach the various destinations the Lord has for them, they will feel a tremendous sense of accomplishment. They will be challenged to attempt bigger and more difficult challenges in discipleship. As their horizons expand, the church is blessed.

But who will lead them in the process of Christian growth and discipleship? The church is in need of leaders who have walked in the footsteps of Christ, who are willing to demonstrate a genuine Christian life.

WHAT DOES A LEADER LOOK LIKE?

One of the most significant mistakes a congregation and its leaders can do is to jump on the small group bandwagon and seek out leaders in a hurried, careless fashion. On the contrary, the best small group ministries are built one healthy leader and group at a time.

Most people are familiar with the phrase *born leader*. While some men and women are so gifted in people skills that they appear to make things just happen, there are many more people who work hard at leadership in various ways. Some of these leaders are highly visible, and some are not so visible. Perhaps some people who consider themselves leaders are not, at least in a Christian sense, while others who do not consider themselves leaders are.

Not all leaders have a positive impact on people's faith. Leaders can deceive, manipulate, control, mislead and more. Also, willingness to lead a small group does not exempt one from making mistakes and causing injury.

Thus, leadership training is imperative. Stimulating the process of spiritual growth requires vigilance and work. Healthy churches provide a leadership structure, accountability and resources for group leaders. Healthy group leaders welcome these provisions, and when they don't have ready access to them (for example, in churches that have not developed such support structures), they seek them out.

Leadership ability is not necessarily something you are born with. It does come more naturally to some people than to others, but most people develop their ability to lead with time and experience.

A good leader is growing in maturity. Mature people know themselves well, are comfortable with what they know, and know how to use their abilities to help others. Others can look at such people and see qualities that they admire and want to imitate. A leader in this mold might not—in fact, often does not—realize how much influence he or she has. That's because a mature leader cares for others without calculating personal gain. This kind of leader will willingly take a back seat when necessary and will mobilize people around Christ instead of around himself or herself.

Leadership has many personalities and gifts. We often think of leaders as outgoing, but many times the quiet leader can develop the full potential of a group of people where the outgoing leader cannot. Leaders assume all types of personalities. In the Gospels we see that Peter usually spoke while the other disciples stood in the background. God used each of the disciples, however, to build his kingdom.

What is true of good leaders is that they carry and apply consistent traits and skills as they serve God and others. This chapter will first examine positive small group leader traits (what you can look for in yourself and in others who may potentially lead) and then describe some of the skills needed in small group ministry (what you may train leaders to apply).

SMALL GROUP LEADER TRAITS

Whenever we attempt to make a list of traits, we confront potential dangers. We face the possibility of imitation, in which prospective leaders will try to manufacture traits that only God can call forth. We face the danger of perfectionism, in which we hold one another to pharisaic standards of performance when in fact God uses broken people to accomplish his purposes. We face the potential for misunderstanding, in which we may miscommunicate about one or more of these traits, when God alone truly understands the complexities of the persons and circumstances that God uses for his will.

Traits of Small Group Leaders

Relationship with God	Personal Life	Relationships with Others
• They think theologically.	• They are aware of their strengths and weaknesses.	• They are nurturing.
• They are humble.	• They are risk-takers.	• They are servants.
	• They are ethical.	

However, if we then choose to not attempt to discern what kinds of traits God uses in leaders, we face the danger of lost focus. Perfection is never a requirement for God's people; being super-pastors is Jesus' role, not ours. Nevertheless, there are several key leadership traits of positive group leadership.

A Christian leader's character is evident in his or her relationship to God. Christian leaders think theologically and are humble. Let's look deeper at these traits.

Theology is the study of God. The starting point for such study is a personal, living relationship with God in Jesus Christ (God revealed in the flesh). A healthy small group leader has accepted God's righteousness in Christ and possesses a desire to know God better.

God's Word is the foundation for all that we do, yet many Christians are woefully ignorant about biblical history, themes and story line. The results carry over into our application of the text, our lifestyle choices, our witness to the world and more.

In fact, in parts of the Western world, and perhaps especially in evangelical Christianity, theology has a bad connotation. Many Christians, including many younger leaders, want stimulating worship, dynamic preaching and teaching, and invigorating nurture programs, and they think of theology as dry, boring, lifeless.

Healthy small group leaders may confess ignorance of God's plan and redemptive history, but they are hungry to know God and willing to do the hard work of Bible study so that they may know God's truth (more on that in chapter eight).

Humility is one of the most difficult virtues to understand; therefore, it is one of the most elusive to grasp. Each human being comes naturally equipped with pride and selfishness, both of which are opposites of humility.

Humility involves a correct understanding of God, others and self. It is rooted in the greatest commandment of all: "Love the Lord your God with all your heart and with all your soul and with all your mind and with all your strength. [And] love your neighbor as yourself. There is no commandment greater than these" (Mk 12:30, 31). Humble people put God first and seek his glory. Then they seek good for others.

I am not advocating a doormat theology here. In fact, a humble person is proud in a positive sense. Truly humble people know what they have to offer and are not scared to give of themselves. As a result, they have the confidence to help others find satisfaction not in worldly rewards but in acts of love. Humility finds its greatest joy in knowing the approval of God the Father.

Too many leaders compete with each other, seeking the world's approval instead of rooting their motivation in God. Rather than moving up in the world, we need to focus on moving ahead in a spiritual sense. There is much more love to go around when leaders are humble.

If we are thinking theologically and practicing humility, evidence of God's work in our lives will be manifest in how we live.

A *Christian leader's character is evident in his or her personal life*. Christian leaders are aware of their strengths and weaknesses, are willing to take risks, and are concerned with the ethics of their leadership.

• *Aware of strengths and weaknesses.* A leader should be self-confident but also realistic. All of us need to be aware of what we do well. We also need to know what we don't do very well. A healthy dose of self-honesty is good for anyone.

Take an inventory of those things you do well, and those things that you do not do so well. You may decide that you talk too much in group situations. One person's dominating the conversation tends to inhibit the growth of the group. Your awareness of this weakness, however, can be useful. You can share your weakness and ask your group to help you, or you can organize group meeting times in such a way that your weakness is minimized.

• *Willing to take risks.* In the parable of the talents (Mt 25:14-30) three servants were given varying amounts of money. Their master then went away and left the servants to themselves. The first two servants invested their talents so that they were able to give the master a great profit when he returned. The third hid his talent, feeling that it would be much safer underground. The master rewarded the first two servants and punished the third.

The message for leaders is obvious. God has given us gifts and abilities for the benefit of ourselves and others. When we use what we have been given for God's purposes, the risk of failure is more than offset by the potential gain.

There are times when small group leaders will be called on to take risks. In a time where group tension is running high, you may need to bring things into the open. Maybe your group gossips about people, and you feel that it is time to confront the issue. Perhaps it is time for your group to think of multiplying or dying, yet you know that bringing up the subject will create conflict.

Strong leaders learn to assess situations, seek out the wisdom of others and act. When failure occurs, that same leader will pick up the pieces and move forward.

• *Concerned with ethics.* Humans tend to build on both mistakes and weaknesses. When we sin, we are prone to take bigger and bigger steps away from God, often without knowing it. The child who snatches one cookie, thinking it won't be noticed, will be tempted to take another. Little "slips" can easily produce a pattern that governs our thinking, followed by bigger slips and finally a fall. Leaders need to be above reproach so that we can foster the kind of respect that our position dictates, which means guarding against small slips as well as big falls.

Why does a strong ethic matter in group life? Because a leader's (and group's) witness is at stake. Imagine a leader who expects all members to do their homework in a timely manner but neglects to do it, and then "fudges" that laziness by pretending to know the material. Eventually, people will discover the inconsistency, and the group will suffer.

Healthy life traits create strong leaders. Sloppy life traits undermine not only leaders but the people they serve.

A Christian leader's character is evident in his or her relationship with others. Christian leaders are nurturing servants. It makes little sense to be a leader without caring about the growth of those who are under your leadership. This is what the process of discipleship is all about.

• *Nurturing*. Good nurturing relationships involve two perspectives. First, a healthy discipling relationship involves complete acceptance of the person being discipled by the disciple-maker. You cannot work with people unless you are willing to accept them, with both good and bad qualities. You will need to pray that you can see them as God sees them—full of potential, and worthy of love and care.

Second, the disciple-maker must provide an atmosphere in which the disciple can grow. Even though leaders accept others as they are, the potential for growth must not be downplayed. On the contrary, when people feel totally accepted they often feel free to start or continue the growth process. The end result of a nurturing relationship is a disciple who becomes more and more like Christ.

• *Serving*. In the Gospels we discover that "the Son of Man came not to be served but to serve" (Mt 20:28 NRSV). We either serve others or we serve ourselves. There is no middle ground.

Consider what Paul writes in Philippians 2. He challenges the Philippians to be like Christ,

> Who, being in very nature God,
> did not consider equality with God something to be grasped,
> but made himself nothing,
> taking the very nature of a servant,
> being made in human likeness. . . .
> He humbled himself
> and became obedient to death —
> even death on a cross! (Phil 2:6-8)

Notice that Jesus recognized his equality with God but was willing to give everything up so that others could benefit. How much more should God's children give up their worldly status to gain in stature as a servant?

A different picture is painted in James 3. In this passage James berates those who call themselves leaders while being selfish and arrogant: "But if you harbor bitter envy and selfish ambition in your hearts, do not boast about it or deny the truth. Such 'wisdom' does not come down from heaven but is earthly, unspiritual, of the devil. For where you have envy and selfish ambition, there you find disorder and every evil practice" (Jas 3:14-16). When we picture leaders like those spoken of in James 3, we begin to understand the confusion that they create.

Many leaders are willing to go into action when their role will be highly visible and offer them glory. The flip side is that we tend to go last when there is no glory to be given us. We love to lead the parade but hate to wrap towels around our waists and wash feet. Christ calls us to be different. Servant leaders will take the lead when things aren't glamorous, and they will be willing to take up the rear when others may benefit during more visible times.

SMALL GROUP LEADER SKILLS

Leadership traits are developed by God, as the Spirit of God works in a person to bring about deeper growth in faith, hope and love. Leadership skills, on the other hand, are developed by a person who practices them. Here are seven key beginning leadership skills that you will need to strengthen as you lead a small group.

- Establishing a covenant
- Understanding group dynamics
- Creating a holistic meeting schedule
- Planning logistics
- Asking good questions
- Sharing group care
- Preparing for future growth

1. A skillful group leader establishes a covenant. Small groups are filled with unique individuals, each bringing a distinct set of assets and problems to the group. Leaders must try to discover, affirm and use the assets, while minimizing the negative impact of potential problems. Such problems can include hidden agendas, desire for control, unhealthy relational interactions and much more.

You may imagine that leaders—absent direction, guidance and structure—might need a host of small, subtle tools to discern and address these problems. Training leaders to recognize situations and use those tools can be a daunting task, but a covenant between members allows leaders to handle many potential group problems before the fact, while offering a vision for the possibility of group health.

Chapter four examines the basics of group covenants (see page 239 for a sample covenant), but generally, a thorough covenant spells out group roles and communication, group expectations and goals, and group dynamics and ground rules. Sadly, studies demonstrate that many existing groups are both unhealthy and operating without covenants. Operating a group without a covenant is similar to running a corporation without a charter, bylaws and strategy.

When I train small group leaders, I am asked how often a covenant should be updated. I usually respond by asking how long it takes the average person to forget what is written on a piece of paper. Most people have short attention spans; therefore, an existing covenant should be reviewed monthly or following vacations and holidays. A new covenant should be negotiated by the group at least every three months.

2. *A skillful group leader understands group dynamics.* All groups possess similar life cycles and traits. For example, every brand new group needs to spend time early in the group's life together developing strong relational bonds. Although the time needed for this unity building varies from group to group, leaders must recognize this group need and devote significant time to building relationships and trust.

Chapters four through seven of this book present a number of issues in group dynamics. Knowing that a group might experience these can be very helpful:

- The four stages of community: *Exploration* (unity at the expense of diversity); *transition* (diversity at the expense of unity); *action* (unity alongside diversity); *termination/multiplication* (affirming unity, bringing a group to an end or forming new groups). As we shall see in chapter seven, leaders who identify these stages are better able to manage the choices and expectations unique to various times in a group's life.

- Healthy group communication patterns, including honesty, affirmation, confidentiality and a no-gossip policy. More on this in chapter four.

- The importance of organization and the planning of positive meetings.

3. *A skillful group leader creates a holistic meeting schedule.* Chapter two covered three elements of a healthy, holistic gathering of Christians: the inward dimension, which includes group care and fellowship; the upward dimension, encompassing prayer, worship and spiritual training; and the outward dimension, including outreach, multiplication, apprenticing and mission.

A practical way to create a holistic group is to design meetings that include all three dimensions.

A Sample Three-Dimensional Meeting Schedule

7:00 p.m.–7:15 p.m.	Inward	Coffee, refreshments, conversation
7:15 p.m.–7:30 p.m.	Inward/Upward	Group sharing or worship
7:30 p.m.–7:45 p.m.	Inward/Upward	Sharing and prayer in groups of four
7:45 p.m.–8:30 p.m.	Upward	Study
8:30 p.m.–8:45 p.m.	Outward	Prayer for outreach, planning for a service project

4. *A skillful group leader plans logistics well.* What do the following items possess in common?

- a dimly lit room with a long, rectangular table
- the smoking section in a noisy restaurant
- an obscure house at the end of five winding roads
- overstuffed couches spread far apart

Each of these items is a small group no-no. Groups need positive relationships to thrive; they also need positive meeting space. The following logistical items should be addressed:

- Where shall we locate our meetings so that the setting is convenient, accessible and reasonable for all participants?

- How can the meeting space be laid out to maximize communication? This category includes placing people in comfortable (not *too* comfortable!) chairs in a circle at a reasonable distance from other individuals, in a quiet space where learning can occur.

- What other meeting rooms are available for subgroupings of four, for fellowship and so on?

- How can we minimize distractions like phone calls, pets or unruly children?

- Who will handle refreshments, and what parameters shall we use (for example, one dessert and several drinks each week, or potluck suppers each week)?

- With what frequency shall we meet (weekly is ideal), and when shall we take breaks (during summer is often helpful)?

5. A skillful group leader asks good questions. One of the greatest assets you can develop is the art of asking questions. Questions keep you from being judgmental, and they allow you to steer clear of conversational roadblocks. Asking questions is helpful for disciples because it allows them to refine issues and requires them to come to grips with the essence of what they are thinking and saying. Through listening, good leaders become better at understanding what is happening with individuals, with the group and with themselves. As James 1:19 puts it, "My dear brothers, take note of this: Everyone should be quick to listen, slow to speak and slow to become angry." This is good advice for the leader, who would do well to cultivate the following skills:

- Ask open-ended questions starting with what, why, how and so on.

- When you ask a question, pause to allow answers. Don't fill empty space too quickly.

- Before you "get into" Bible study, ask a few opener questions (based on people's past, present or future; see chapter five) that will help people (a) get to know each other and (b) prepare to study the text. Many leaders find it helpful to encourage each person to briefly and simply answer each question. Here's an example of an opener question: "You can see that we are studying the story of Nicodemus this evening. When was a time in your childhood or adolescence that you were embarrassed or ashamed of something good?"

- Supplement a Bible study guide with good, probing questions that you may ask of a text. Another name for a probing question is an "I'm just curious . . . " question. We'll talk more about these questions in chapter eight.

6. *A skillful group leader shares group care.* Many leaders take up the mantle of group care as if it were solely their job. Several biblical concepts refute that way of thinking.

First, the "one another" teachings of the New Testament operate under the assumption that each person ministers to others. Second, from the various passages that teach about spiritual gifts (such as 1 Cor 12 and Eph 4) we may assume that the relational gifts (for example, compassion and discernment) are scattered throughout a group. Thus, a leader who assumes those gifts may be "stealing" members' ability to use their gifts by showing care. Third, the wealth of teaching about Christ-centered relationships directs us to be in rich community with each other so that we may practice Christlike love. (See, for instance, the passage in Phil 2 advising us to "consider others better than yourselves.")

Chapters five through seven examine in greater detail some of the following ways that groups may show care and concern to their members:

- maintaining contact during the week through prayer partners, e-mail or bulletin board formats, phone calls, and so on

- praying for each member regularly, especially during intense times of hurt and pain

- listening (when appropriate) and offering sensitive advice in relation to the stresses and past hurts that may be shared

- celebrating special days, such as birthdays, anniversaries and group milestones

- sharing resources (for example, when a member's car breaks down) or providing help during crisis (for example, baby-sitting when a member has a sick spouse)

7. A *skillful group leader prepares to grow*. Psychologist M. Scott Peck writes the following in his intriguing book *The Different Drum: Community Making and Peace* (Simon & Schuster, 1987):

> Community is and must be inclusive. The great enemy of community is exclusivity. Groups that exclude others because they are poor or doubters or divorced or sinners or of some different race or nationality are not communities; they are cliques—actually defensive bastions against community.

The dominant characteristic of a clique (an unhealthy group) is exclusivity, which rationalizes itself in many ways, with comments such as this: "I just need this group for me; let's not invite others in." Exclusivity does not just exist between group members and "outsiders." Exclusivity becomes a mindset that creates mind games, rejection and a host of other subtle gestures within groups themselves. The best antidote for exclusivity is an intentional group understanding that each member of the group exists in ministry within the group, and for ministry outside the group. Leaders such as Darrell Guder of Princeton Theological Seminary have labeled this group understanding the "missional church mindset."

Chapters eleven and twelve will more fully develop some of the ways for groups to be inclusive, among them

- prayer for the empty chair
- targeted prayer for nonbelievers
- service to the church body
- service evangelism
- multiplication
- evangelistic groups

Another key factor in group growth is the use of a group apprentice. An apprentice is a leader in training. If your group is healthy and growing, then an apprentice can be trained to do the very things the leader does, so that he or she will be in a position to help bring a new group into being.

FREEDOM TO FALL GRACEFULLY

If you're a prospective leader, you might be intimidated by all that you're being told you need to learn to be a skillful group leader. Some might become paralyzed by the thought *What if I fail?*

The most liberating thing about the gospel is that it provides a solution for failure. If you were a humanist, who believed that human beings represent the world's highest potential, and you failed at something important, where would you turn? There would be nowhere to go for help except to other failing humans. As Christians, we know that human beings are always failing and live in constant need of God, *and* we can go to God. We can tell God about our failures and ask him to forgive us and help us to go on. In response, God tells us, "Yes, I saw that. You did blow it. But Jesus' sacrifice on the cross is enough to cover your mistake. Consider it a closed issue. Go and don't do it anymore. I still love you." This is what the Bible calls grace—undeserved favor.

Imagine how tormented Peter felt when he came to his senses in the temple courtyard and realized that he had publicly disowned Jesus, his Master and friend, during Jesus' most difficult hour (Jn 18:15-18, 25-26). Only a few days later, however, he ate breakfast with Jesus on the beach, and their relationship was restored (Jn 21:1-19). Think how relieved Peter must have been to receive forgiveness from Jesus. Few disciples had blown it worse than Peter, and few disciples went on to become more useful to God. In spite of failure, God's grace allows us to move on as disciples.

Also remember what Paul wrote:

> Not that I have already obtained all this, or have already been made perfect, but I press on to take hold of that for which Christ Jesus took hold of me. Brothers, I do not consider myself yet to have taken hold of it. But one thing I do: Forgetting what is behind and straining toward what is ahead, I press on toward the goal to win the prize for which God has called me heavenward in Christ Jesus. All of us who are mature should take such a view of things. And if on some point you think differently, that too God will make clear to you. Only let us live up to what we have already attained. (Phil 3:12-16)

Knowing this, with God's help, are you willing to be a small group leader who becomes a disciple-maker? And more important, are you willing to be a growing disciple?

QUESTIONS FOR REVIEW

1. What is the point of the rappelling story in the beginning of the chapter?

1. Give some examples of leaders who are like the "leader" in that story.

2. Give some examples of leaders who are the opposite of the leader in that story.

3. What, in your own words, is a leader?

4. How do you feel about yourself in relation to your definition of a leader?

5. What leadership traits do you feel you possess? What traits does God need to make stronger in you?

6. Review the seven skills for leaders. What skills do you feel good about? Which ones do you need to work on?

READING FOR REFLECTION

- A leadership training resource with accompanying tape: *Nine Keys to Effective Small Group Leadership* by Carl George (Kingdom Publishing).

- Several leadership resources from NavPress/Pilgrimage Training Group: *Small Group Fitness Kit* by Thom Corrigan; *Seven Traits of Healthy Leaders* and *Seven Tools for Effective Leaders* by Jeff Arnold.

IDEAS FOR COACHES/TRAINERS

Imagine that you are preparing to start a small group. Discuss the potential leadership issues and pitfalls, and how to address them, when starting a group consisting of the following people:

- blue-collar men
- older women
- mixed singles and married couples
- people from a wide range of ages
- university professors

Spend time going over your church's strategy concerning leadership development, training and ongoing support.

4

STARTING A GROUP

Hi, Brett, Heather, Hannah and Karen.

"Maybe you're wondering why I've called you together this evening. Well, I was recently an apprentice leader in a small group, and I've just finished a course on being a small group leader. I now feel that I should start a small group.

"What do we do in a small group, you ask? Well, to be quite frank, I have no idea what to do next. If you will just wait, I'll flip through my training manual and see what I should do. Let's see, do I find it under the chapter on Bible study or the one on community building? I have no idea. I'm so embarrassed. I guess we should just end this meeting now. I hope to see you next week at the same time."

Leading a small group can be difficult. You may find yourself preparing to start a first group and realize how scared you are. You have rehearsed what you will say many times, but each time you end up telling the group that you don't know what you are doing.

It's like driving. You can watch others drive and may even have opinions about their competence. But when you first get behind the wheel, it's a little awkward. Movements that become second nature with time make you feel self-conscious at first.

That's how you might feel about being a small group leader. If you've been in a group or two before, you probably have ideas about how to make your group more effective, but you are now being called on to assume leadership for a group. And you want to do a good job. You want to make disciples and create a loving community within which your group can study, pray, worship and reach out to the world. But where do you start? This chapter examines logistic and leadership issues necessary to start your first small group.

GATHERING GROUP MEMBERS

The first step is to pull together a small group of disciples who are willing to grow under your leadership. The place to start, when attempting to gather a group, is on your knees. In Luke 6:12-16 we read that before Jesus chose those who would follow him for the next few years, he committed the choice to his heavenly Father.

There are a number of reasons this is important for us. First, if Jesus sought God's help in pulling a group together, how much more do we need God's guidance? Second, if you start a ministry in prayer, it is easier to remember what you are doing and why you are doing it. Third, only God is in charge of the thousands of intangibles that affect how a ministry occurs. Who else could work within so many personalities, relationships, means of communication, expectations, and insecurities to produce a good result? We should not fool ourselves—only God has the power to bring blessing from our efforts. We must offer ourselves to God and then ask him to mold and shape our work so that his kingdom benefits.

You have several factors to consider when forming a group. For example, your church or fellowship may have a specific means of placing people into groups. In some churches, a coordinator will put together the small groups. Especially in large churches, this may happen out of necessity.

In most cases, however, it is best for small group leaders to choose their own people. This is because you must have a clear idea of the kinds of people you can work with and will feel most comfortable leading. If you make the choices, then you will be more likely to make the best of all situations.

If you are putting together a small group "from scratch," you must discern whom to invite. Part of the answer to this question depends on what kind of group you will be leading (we'll consider various types of groups in this chapter). You may also want to keep in mind who would make a good apprentice leader (more on this in chapter eleven) and host or hostess of the group.

There should ultimately be only one significant prerequisite for membership in your small group—*willingness* to be a disciple. Even evangelistic small groups need a core of dedicated disciples. If a person is not willing to grow, you will only encounter great frustration.

This doesn't mean that you only choose high-profile church members to be in your group. On the contrary, you may not be aware how many people you are in contact with who would love to be invited into a group. As you and the others starting the group with you pray and seek individuals for your group, consider people from your circle of influence—your congregation, neighborhood, workplace and even family.

You might wonder how best to make contact with prospective new members. The best means of drawing persons into groups is by face-to-face contact. An initial invitation can be followed up by a phone call and, as the first meeting nears, perhaps a card with directions to the meeting location.

One way that you will discover willingness to grow (and there is no sure way) is by presenting the challenge of discipleship to a person. You could say something like this: "I know you fairly well, and one thing that I think I see in you is a desire to grow closer to God. I want to grow, too, and am wondering if you would like to meet with me, and possibly a few others, on a weekly basis. We would get together and help each other to grow in our faith."

You will find that some respond very strongly to this challenge (and they tend to thrive in group settings) and others hesitate. If you can get a few people who accept the challenge, then you are ready to go forward with your first meeting.

Here's a general rule of thumb when you are not gathering in a location well known to all members, such as an individual member's home or a restaurant. Have members (at least those requiring help) meet in a central location, and then drive together. This will accomplish several things: First, if people know you are waiting for them, they will be more prone to come, and on time; second, you ensure that people do not get lost, a hindrance to future attendance; and third, you demonstrate that the leader cares about people and details, building trust for the future.

Once individuals have accepted your invitation, the real work of ministry begins. Now the small group must begin to solve the problem of its identity. It is at this time that the group starts to consider who they are and what they do. To guide your group and to teach healthy group life, a group covenant is your best means of communicating these issues.

BUILDING A COVENANT

Starting in Genesis 1 ("Be fruitful, and multiply . . ."), and continuing throughout Scripture ("This is the new covenant of my blood . . ."),

God is depicted as our covenant God. This simply means that he chooses to communicate with us in the form of a set of promises (a covenant). Through the creation covenant, the subsequent covenants with Noah, Abraham, Moses, and David, and then the New Testament covenant of communion, we learn of God's grace and the responsibilities that are ours as God's chosen people.

Covenants exist in a domain far beyond the God-human relationship. We constantly engage in covenant building and enforcing—necessary because of human frailty and sin. When we purchase a house or car, we sign a covenant (a contract). When we sign up for life or health insurance, purchase an airline ticket or cruise, and even go through a checkout line at the grocery store, we receive some document that stipulates what we pay and what we receive. When we open a box of cereal, and the contents are stale, we can read the cereal box for information about how to receive a refund—a form of a covenant.

Ironically, although we would never allow ourselves to be so naïve as to purchase a major item without an agreement of some sort, Christians tend to engage in many activities without first agreeing to fundamental issues that define our relationships. For example, most church committees do not have covenants. Newcomers are somehow supposed to figure out their roles and the function of the group they have joined. In the absence of clear direction and vision, many churches experience conflict and strife as various individuals or groups attempt to create and enforce unspoken covenant rules. What they may not realize is that they simply need to sit down together, affirm some basic ground rules, and negotiate vision and strategy issues.

Unless you are going to assume leadership of an existing group, some time in the early life of the group, usually in the first meeting, you should present the group with its first covenant, prepared by you (and your coleaders, if applicable). The reason you present the first covenant is because brand new groups have not yet worked and learned together, and perhaps they need education in basic small group issues. These first covenants are not meant to last for long, usually four to six weeks. This covenant will help the group identify itself and its purpose, and it will help hold the individuals accountable to the group (see page 239 for a sample first covenant). Appendix A includes a four-week small group beginner guide, which includes a first covenant and has the initial small group experiences laid out in such a way that the covenant is affirmed and taught.

WHAT DOES A COVENANT STIPULATE?

Covenants stipulate the mutual expectations and responsibilities involved when we participate in a transaction or relationship between at least two parties. When covenant writing is part of a healthy group pattern, everyone is allowed equal input, and the success of the group ultimately lies with each individual attempting to meet the expectations laid down and agreed to by all.

When preparing a covenant, group consensus is crucial. Consensus actually provides an unequal vote weighting in the interest of protecting each individual's group participation. This means that, on negotiable matters of group life (as we shall see shortly, some matters are to be nonnegotiable, including those that contribute to group health), one individual unable or unwilling to comply with a particular item has the ability to call the group to reconsider and change that item. For example, if everyone in the group wants to do an intensive study of the book of Revelation, but one member feels she cannot complete the homework on a weekly basis, the group will reopen the conversation and seek an alternative.

When writing a group covenant, you will want to consider identity issues (who we are); task issues (what we do); communication issues (how we interact); and role issues (who does what).

IDENTITY ISSUES: WHO ARE WE?

You have probably been in contact with groups that have been meeting together for a long time. You can hear them discussing their identity when they get together, saying things like, "Remember how Jim pushed Martha in the snow on our second ski trip? That was so funny, even though Martha didn't speak to him for the rest of the weekend. Can you believe that they're married now?" A good part of the group identity is discovered through life experience.

The group will determine part of its identity each time it meets, for each relational time brings a greater experience of community. Some questions, though, need to be answered within a short time after the group has gotten together. If these foundational issues of identity are answered clearly and properly, the group will be free to explore its relationship within safe parameters.

What kind of small group will we be? You can choose from a number of different types of groups when ministering to different needs within a church.

For a sampling of various group types, see pages 76-80. The various group descriptions are helpful because they give guidance in choosing a particular group focus. At the same time, the lines between different group types cannot be clearly drawn. For example, a ministry group might look very much like a cell group, and vice versa. Every small group possesses its own character, and it is impossible to fit a group into a particular category without ignoring some of its personality.

Who can be in the group? At first this question will be answered mostly by you, as you choose your group (in consultation with your apprentice and group host or hostess).

While recruiting members, you should keep in mind that they would like to know what they are getting themselves into. It is helpful to share with each prospective member the names of others you hope to invite into the group. Some groups are formed by recruiting a certain kind of person (gender groups, affinity groups, high-level commitment groups).

What are our attendance expectations? People need to know what is expected of them. Even if everyone assumes that they will attend every meeting, it is helpful for the group to make this commitment to each other. In this way, they will feel more comfortable in their new relationship. Someone who skips a meeting will know that he or she is missed by the group (and will be called) and will be more committed to the other members as a result.

Who can join the group? When and how? Biblical, biological and sociological evidence strongly suggests that healthy groups grow. Some small groups may feel spiritually strong while remaining the same for an extended period of time, but in chapters eleven and twelve we make the point that maturing Christians share their faith and touch a hurting world with the love of Jesus. Successful church small group models in operation today assume that groups will grow and multiply.

Group dynamics change with each new member. Before new people join the group, the whole small group needs to make a commitment to grow. Group experts typically refer to this choice as an "open group" (as opposed to a "closed group" or a non-inviting group).

If you decide to be an open group, you might still decide to close the group during certain periods of time before taking on new members—to be an open/closed group. Or you might make a commitment to grow only through evangelism (not a bad commitment!).

Then, the group should recognize that it may need to multiply into two groups if it gets above a certain size (usually ten to twelve is considered a good size for multiplication). If you nurture an apprentice leader from within your group, that person will want the opportunity to lead. Others will desire to support the new leader, and a group birth can occur with very happy results. There will still be the pain of separation from the main group, but the pain is more than offset by the joy of knowing that the groups are growing and making a difference. Discipleship is not to be hoarded; it is to be shared.

Group logistics. The group must also know such things as where and when they are going to meet. Will you meet in a home, or at the church? Will you meet weekly or once every other week? What about refreshments? Outside activities? What will you do with children? Discipline of children? Pets? Phone calls during the meeting?

If you don't understand the importance of group logistics, try this exercise. Hold a meeting in a cold, dimly lit room with saggy furniture. Make sure that the room is filled with cats (for those who might be allergic), cell phones (set to go off at strategic times) and children (wandering around with diapers sagging). Arrange the chairs into a square, so that each person faces outward rather than inward. Then sit back and watch the group!

Details and logistics matter greatly. If a room is too large, the group gets lost; if it is too small, the group feels uncomfortable. Both realities change the way that people interact with each other. So, for example, if you choose to rotate home meeting places, discuss how to minimize distractions while maximizing interaction (positive meeting spaces, well lit, every person can make eye contact, and so on).

You should choose to meet in a home or location that has a comfortable room with the best possibility for uninterrupted time. The general principle to remember is that you need to arrange your time so that community building and discipleship can occur. If refreshments are a distraction, don't have them. If children are a distraction, find creative ways to keep them occupied. Minimize phone calls (you might leave the phone on for emergencies).

TASK ISSUES: WHAT WILL WE DO?

A second key section of the group covenant describes the manner in which the group will use its time together. For this section, it is helpful to adopt our inward/upward/outward rubric of the previous two chapters. Every healthy group, no matter what its focus, will possess some element of each of these three.

For example, when a typical group is just getting started, its leaders usually want the group members to get to know each other and develop a bond of love (inward). Does that mean the group doesn't use a study (upward)? Of course not. And by the same token, although we can assume a three-week-old group is not ready to multiply (outward), they may be ready to plan service projects, or to place an empty chair in the group circle and pray for the (most likely unknown) person who will sometime in the future be invited to fill that chair. Table 4.1 offers a sample of what a three-week-old group meeting might look like.

Table 4.1. Meeting Structure After Three Weeks

7:00–7:15 p.m.	Group mingling, refreshments
7:15–7:30 p.m.	Opening prayer, prayer for empty chair
7:30–8:00 p.m.	Ice breaker, community building
8:00–8:30 p.m.	Singing, study time
8:30–8:45 p.m.	Prayer requests, closing prayer

COMMUNICATION ISSUES: WHAT ARE OUR GROUND RULES?

Once you have set the functional identity questions, you can establish group communication rules. In groups with good communication patterns from the start, they are perhaps unnecessary. But in many groups there are people who dominate, belittle or take over discussions. For these reasons, a few ground rules could be helpful. Here is a list of possibilities:

- We will keep what is said in the group between group members (confidentiality).
- We will not put people down for what they say.
- We will not allow one person to dominate.
- We will try to be as honest as possible with each other within this group.
- We will not talk about others behind their backs.
- We will not gossip about people who are outside the group.

No matter how you choose to "enforce" these ground rules, they are helpful. The purpose of the ground rules is to keep Christ-centered, edifying talk in the group meetings.

GROUP ROLE ISSUES: WHO WILL DO WHAT?

Finally, a group covenant identifies different group roles, and who fills them. Such an overt placement of leadership allows the group to forego the subtle power games that often play out beneath the surface of group life.

In chapter seven we will examine such roles in greater detail. Of course, there will be a group leader. Then, you might have an apprentice leader to train and prepare for leadership. We have also mentioned a host or hostess (a small hint: if you lead the group, it is often best to have the meeting in another place than where you live, so that you can concentrate on the group and not worry about the meeting atmosphere). Other roles can fill perceived group needs: prayer leader; fellowship/event coordinator; outreach coordinator; and so forth.

THREE STAGES OF GROUP DEVELOPMENT

From the outset you may find it helpful to discern the differences between groups just getting started, groups that are maturing and groups that are preparing to disband.

Just getting started. This is the time in a group's life, usually in its first three months, when the group is trying to discover its identity. In the very beginning, the idea of a small group existing is in itself a unifying factor. What does the group do during this time? *The primary focus of the group is building community.* The group will not grow if it does not come together into a unified, loving fellowship of believers. The most important thing that the group can do is to plan activities and lessons in such a way that the group gets to know each of its individuals in a deeper way. A good community building resource for this stage can be found in appendix A.

Leaders should take a direct, hands-on approach to leadership during this time. This will free up the individual members to pursue relationships within the group. As the group matures, leaders can give responsibility to those who are prepared to handle it.

For example, in the first meeting, you might want to share your vision for small group ministry and ask others in the group for theirs. In the second, you may want to help the group think through the group covenant. In the next meetings, you will want to see that the covenant is enforced and revised, so that the group starts running smoothly. And only then can you expect to get others involved in the leadership of the group.

Make sure that the covenant is clear and comprehensive. It is important that the group covenant matches what actually happens in the group. For this reason you may want to write your initial covenant for a trial period, perhaps for six weeks. Then you can re-evaluate and adjust the covenant as the group desires.

Mature group. Once a group understands its identity and has worked through the first stages of its group life, it can then be classified as "mature." A mature group is one that is usually older than three months and younger than two years (although a healthy mature group can last indefinitely). What marks a group's maturity is not so much how long it's been together, as how effectively it is able to focus on its primary task(s). A mature group moves from establishing community to building strong disciples (upward dimension) and sharing God's love in Christ with the world (outward).

In a mature group you should never stop focusing on community. Community is a key structure your group will learn and grow in. Participation in social activities, service projects, dinners and outreach activities is perhaps more important as friendships deepen than at any time before. With deeper relationships comes a greater desire to be together.

At this point the group is able to focus spiritual maturity. If you have a regular cell group, then prayer, Bible study and outreach will start taking a greater share of group time. With a mission group, maturity brings more creativity and effective ministry. Moving to maturity means that any group can become better at what it originally contracted to become. *As the group experiences God's blessing, it will start to want to share that blessing with others.* You can, and should, start encouraging the group to identify with God's plan to bring salvation to others through his children.

In a mature group, leadership development and potential parent-child multiplication issues will surface. Your role as leader should evolve from hands-on functional leadership to friendship and leadership development. As the group matures, you will empower members in the group to take responsibility for various group activities. In addition, you can seek positive group apprentice leaders whom you can prepare for their own small group leadership. Perhaps you can take them through this book yourself and encourage them to take a few of the "parent" group's members and start their own "child" group. In this way, you will avoid the stagnation that accompanies ingrown groups and can allow your own group to remain at a size that encourages it to grow.

Indeed, in theory at least, mature groups need never move to the final stage of group life. If your group is able to multiply, and then the new groups are able to continue multiplying within two years, you can effectively create mature groups without having to bring those groups to a termination stage.

Later group. Later groups are preparing to terminate. In a highly mobile society like ours, this is in part caused by group members moving. Nonmultiplying groups lasting more than one or two years are the exception, not the rule.

Terminating a group requires skill and strong leadership. Many groups preparing to terminate are no doubt tempted to simply walk away without dealing with the sadness and grief that may accompany such a stage. However, a terminating group provides yet another teaching moment, and you will want to assert yourself in bringing people together for at least one more meeting or set of meetings.

There is no exciting way to terminate, but there are effective ways to prepare. Some groups terminate by holding one last meeting, a party, and offering people the opportunity to share how their lives have been impacted by the group. Other groups (for example, some groups that are preparing to multiply but whose members are hesitant to part ways) prepare for termination by meeting with less frequency, like once per month or every other week. Over time, the group will naturally draw apart, and the end of the group will be less painful than it might otherwise be.

LEADERSHIP RESPONSIBILITIES

Perhaps you feel overwhelmed at the task that you face. Leadership is not to be taken lightly, and for that reason small group coordinators must recruit the best people that they can find. Small group leaders face a significant test of their ability and character. Here, in short form, is a list of responsibilities that leaders should fulfill:

- Pray.
- Maintain the focus.
- Develop your own growth and leadership.
- Recruit your group (or work with the small group coordinator in your church).
- Coordinate and lead group meetings and activities.
- Help the group develop a group covenant.
- Develop leaders from within the group.
- Prepare the group for outreach and multiplication.
- Evaluate as necessary.
- Continue to pray at all times.

GROUP TYPES

In the section that follows we will examine some of the different types of small groups you may choose to lead.

Cell Group (also known as Care Group or Home Group)

- Description: This group type includes a broad focus which can,

over the life of the group, include all of the emphases discussed in
this book. The group typically gathers for the purpose of community building, personal and corporate growth, and ultimately, multiplication.

- Focus: Individual care; community building; Bible study, worship and prayer; evangelism and mission.

- Membership Profile: Anyone within the church can become associated with a cell group, provided he or she is willing to grow
  and is able to fulfill the disciplines required by a particular group.

- Strengths and Weaknesses: This is probably the most common
  group to be found in the church—for good reason. People grow
  in an atmosphere of love, and they are challenged with the claims
  of Christ. Evangelism and mission, in the form of multiplication,
  should be intentionally built into the group over time.

Discipleship Group

- Description: The word *discipleship* means different things to different people. My emphasis is on the intense relationship that Jesus
  had with his disciples. A discipleship group tends to be small (two
  to four members) and focused on personal and spiritual growth. It
  is ministry-oriented only in the sense that those who have been
  "discipled" are free to go forth and minister because they have been
  empowered in their relationship to God and others.

- Focus: Individual care; community building; Bible study, worship and prayer.

- Membership Profile: This group is for those who are very serious
  about their faith and who are not afraid to make a deep commitment to relational accountability.

- Strengths and Weaknesses: Discipleship groups are very exciting, transforming lukewarm Christians into people of God. To avoid becoming ingrown, stagnant and exclusive, there should be a definite starting and stopping point to the relationship.

Ministry Group

- Description: As its name implies, this type of group focuses on ministry, evangelism and mission. It can take the form of a committee, a working group (like a group of carpenters committed to restoring broken-down homes for the homeless), or a small group that regularly engages in ministry or evangelism.

- Focus: Individual care; community building; mission; possibly study, worship or prayer ministry; evangelism.

- Membership Profile: Church committees (like the mission committee, evangelism and discipleship committees, or Christian education committee) can become ministry groups by reorienting their typical ministry focus to include discipleship-community building for member-equipping purposes. Small groups can form or reform for the purpose of evangelism or mission. This group type is for those who have a burden to make a difference for Christ in the world.

- Strengths and Weaknesses: If not organized properly, these groups can become overly focused on task and can lose their direction. Groups need a specific covenant so that roles and member responsibilities are clearly defined. Leaders must have a vision for both discipleship and outreach, or the group will lose its reason for existence. Everyone in the group should help formulate the group focus and vision so that all have ownership in the ministry, evangelism or mission.

Special-Needs Group

- Description: The church can be viewed as a hospital, helping people to become whole in relation to self, others and God. Special-needs groups place the primary emphasis on this kind of relational and emotional healing.

- Focus: Individual care and healing; community building; outreach to others who are broken; possibly study, worship and prayer.

- Membership Profile: Groups like Alcoholics Anonymous, Al-Anon, Overeaters Anonymous, and other "12-step" groups are special-needs groups. Because they usually minister to a specific need (like alcoholism), a church could have any number of these groups.

- Strengths and Weaknesses: Observing the explosion of 12-step groups across the country, it is obvious that important needs are being met. Churches can become involved by initiating Christian special-needs groups, building a bridge from the church to a community in need. Over time, people in 12-step groups can be assimilated into a church.

Affinity Group

- Description: An affinity group is a gathering of people who possess a common interest or characteristic. Young mothers, teachers, young people, singles and businesspeople are all examples of people who naturally relate to others in their subgroup. A businesswoman may want to gather other businesswomen at her place of employment for mutual support and growth in Christ. Affinity groups can spring up anywhere anytime (including Sunday school) that people have a common bond and a desire to grow in Christ.

- Focus: Individual care; community building; Bible study, worship and prayer; evangelism and mission.

- Membership Profile: There are almost a limitless number of potential affinity groups that can be formed. An affinity group exists when people of similar race, sex or circumstance come together for the purpose of mutual support and growth in discipleship.

- Strengths and Weaknesses: A group like this has the same strengths and weaknesses as a cell group. In addition, there is the added strength that comes from sharing the Christian life with others who can understand. The affinity group's strength is also its weakness. If people only get together with others of similar circumstance, much of the learning that could take place in the church is stunted. You can learn just as much, if not more, from those in different situations.

House Church

- Description: The house church functions just like a church that is held in the home. The group meeting time typically includes a full worship service and a fellowship time before or after the service. The small group leader who leads this type of group becomes the "church's" pastor, a position of great honor and responsibility.

- Focus: Individual care; worship, prayer and Bible study; outreach.

- Membership Profile: Same as that of a typical cell group—anyone with a desire to grow in Christ.

- Strengths and Weaknesses: A well-planned, member-involving worship service can be valuable for stimulating Christian growth. On the negative side, the potential exists for the "spectator complex" to take over, thus inhibiting the small group's natural ability to engage all members in Christian growth and learning.

QUESTIONS FOR REVIEW

1. What are your greatest concerns as you prepare to lead a small group? How will you address your concerns?

2. What part does, and should, prayer play in your decision making?

3. What is the most important prerequisite for membership in small groups, and why?

4. Why is it important for groups to determine identity issues?

5. What is the role of ground rules?

6. How do you feel about your leadership readiness?

7. What are key distinctives involved in leading a group just starting to meet? A mature group? A group preparing to disband or multiply?

8. Look over the different group types on pages 76-80. What kind of group do you expect to lead? Who will you ask to be in your group?

READING FOR REFLECTION

- For a resource full of ideas for leading groups, see *The Willow Creek Guide to Leading Life-Changing Small Groups* (Zondervan) by Bill Donahue.

- An older resource that examines Jesus' method of making disciples is Robert Coleman's *The Master Plan of Evangelism* (Revell).

IDEAS FOR COACHES/TRAINERS

- Brainstorm what you believe to be the five most significant criticisms that could be made of small groups (for example, they promote cliques).

- Discuss how the group covenant might address these criticisms and promote healthy group life.

- Revisit the church's material; if a covenant is supplied, go over it. You may also discuss how people are placed into groups.

THE BUILDING BLOCKS OF COMMUNITY

Mission control to small group: We have engaged all engines, and blast-off has been a success. Have a great trip!

DESTINATION: DISCIPLESHIP

Nothing good and lasting can occur without thoughtful planning and preparation. Consider how much time and energy goes into the launching of one space shuttle. Companies all over the world assemble the various components while a team of scientists, physicists, engineers and managers prepares to pull everything together into a working vehicle. As experience has shown, one flaw can be fatal. The responsibility given to the team of designers and builders is tremendous.

Yet a successfully launched spaceship provides awe-inspiring drama to observers. Workers who develop and build these vehicles receive tremendous satisfaction. A team that sees its work resulting in space walks, or photographs from faraway planets, has much to be proud of.

People at NASA and in other space programs around the world are always reaching for the next planet or star. People who lead small groups should aim high as well. We started this training course by showing you your destination—to make disciples of all people in multiplying cells. Picture your small group ministry reaching many in your church, town or state with the unique claims of Jesus Christ.

Knowing where you are going is helpful; but equally important, you must understand how you will arrive at your destination. We may think of a spaceship as the most important component, or structure, for reaching a faraway planet. For groups, that structure is a caring community, something we will learn about in this chapter and chapters six and seven.

THE FELLOWSHIP HOUR

You know the routine. You walk out of the sanctuary on Sunday morning, shake the pastor's hand, take a left down the hall, and enter the fellowship hall. You make small talk with people as you stand in line for a cup of coffee, and then you spend the next thirty minutes mingling with your friends from the church. When you feel a tug on your sleeve, you are reminded by your youngest child that you must leave. You round up everyone, load the car and head for home.

The fellowship hour, whether before or after church, is often an indispensable part of a church's life. In fact, in some churches, fellowship hour is almost as important as the worship hour. These times provide value because people become acquainted through normal conversation. By attending a fellowship hour, people can feel loved and accepted just because people are willing to spend time with them.

Others, however, may not feel so positive about the fellowship hour. Some people who leave church fellowship times feel sad, ignored or rejected. Maybe they were struggling with something and nobody asked about their problem. Perhaps they were shy and few people came over to talk to them. Informal fellowship time does not tend to offer help for those kinds of needs.

The limitations of the fellowship hour are magnified by societal changes brought by technology and mobility. The mobility brought by the automobile and superhighways has created social disconnection from primary family and societal relationships. The entertainment provided by the television has dulled senses and creativity, thus limiting individuals' problem-solving abilities. The efficiency and information brought by the computer has created fewer relational interactions, resulting in isolation. The challenges of maintaining economic prosperity have created more work hours and less family time.

Many leaders, including teachers, counselors, college administrators and pastors, have noticed that individuals today bring much emotional and relational "baggage." People feel disconnected, uncertain and unprepared. In the sociological environment of the early twenty-first century, small groups can become the avenue for deep healing. They can become a greenhouse for community, a safe place to learn relational skills. In order to understand how they may accomplish this healing, however, we must understand more about Christian community.

THEY BROKE BREAD TOGETHER

Many people turn to the famous passage in Acts 2:42-47 to provide a snapshot of community in the early church. It is a wonderful passage, full of people spending time together—praying, talking, eating and worshiping. It would have been very exciting to be a part of the Jerusalem Christian Church during the early days of church growth after the Holy Spirit had been given. Acts 2 is helpful because it shows how a group of people who wanted to be faithful to Christ attempted to grow in discipleship together. Any fellowship would do well to take the principles that they operated with and put them to use in their own community of faith.

There is no passage in the Bible that says, "You must have a small group for people to grow in their faith." Instead, what is in the Bible is an understanding, from beginning to end, that people need an authentic, intimate community in which to grow. In the Scriptures, a community is a group of people, living under God's rule, who are learning how to love God and love one another.

The community of Israel. The Old Testament is very much the story of a community, Israel. Genesis shows how God promised Abraham, Israel's forefather, that he would bring blessing to the whole world through a nation that would come from his seed. The people of Israel were enslaved in Egypt, and then released by God's intervention. In the Book of Exodus, God's purpose for Israel becomes very clear. He had chosen Israel so that he could build a community of faith that would influence other nations for his glory (Ex 33:15-16). This community would live under God's Law, helping each other to love and serve God with heart, soul, mind and strength.

The promises contained in the Law (Exodus, Leviticus and Deuteronomy) existed for the whole nation, and the curses were for the whole nation as well. In fact, because the community was linked so intimately together, it would rise and fall together. When God saw Israel, he saw a whole, a community. When the community was obedient to God and loving toward each other, he blessed them. When they were disobedient to God and they oppressed each other, he removed his presence from them, and they were punished.

In the end, the community of faith became a society of sin. Sadly, the Israelite nation ended up dispersed and defeated. But God never lost the vision for what a positive, God-centered community could do.

A new community. In the New Testament we learn about a new community beginning with the faith community that surrounded Jesus. The book of Acts traces the development of the New Testament church, depicting a cohesive, forward-looking church (though not without problems). Other New Testament books, seeking to build a caring, interrelated community, encourage believers to love each other according to Christ's example.

Perhaps no New Testament book makes a clearer statement on Christian fellowship than Ephesians. We read these words about God's plan:

> He came and preached peace to you who were far away and peace to those who were near. For through him we both have access to the Father by one Spirit. Consequently, you are no longer foreigners and aliens, but fellow citizens with God's people and members of God's household. . . . And in him you too are being built together to become a dwelling in which God lives by his Spirit. (Eph 2:17-19, 22)

From this passage we discover the first basic principle undergirding community—people of different backgrounds have been brought together through the salvation offered in Jesus Christ. The common bond that links Christians together is not the similarity of our past, but the convergence of our future. We are family, now and forever.

The second principle can be found in Ephesians 5:1-2: "Be imitators of God, therefore, as dearly loved children and live a life of love, just as Christ loved us and gave himself up for us as a fragrant offering and sacrifice to God." Thus, the Christian community is a place where we can start to practice the Christian life together. Community offers a place where we can succeed and fail in an atmosphere of acceptance and adherence to God's law.

The third principle is found late in the same passage from Ephesians. We are commanded to love each other as Christ loved us. A Christian community is a place to learn about unselfish, kind, patient, trustworthy love. As we experience the love of other Christians, we experience the wonderful love of God.

To summarize, in Christian community, believers are brought together to learn obedience to Christ in an atmosphere of acceptance and love. How do small groups fit into this plan for community?

Priority has been given to developing a biblical concept of community because, while we don't necessarily find a biblical imperative for the formation of a small group ministry, we do find the concepts of discipleship and community in Scripture. It is through small groups that these twin imperatives are best served.

DIVERSITY AND UNITY

If you look again at our definition of community (*in Christian community, believers are brought together to become better disciples of Christ in an atmosphere of acceptance and love*), you can isolate a key issue related to community building. The issue is how to bring together various individuals, with their different pasts and needs, into a functioning, effective body going in one direction. In other words, there are many different parts to a rocket, so how do you put them together so that it can effectively fly as one vehicle?

The solution is not simple, and you will stretch your leadership ability as you wrestle with this issue in your own small group. In this chapter and chapter six we will consider how to minister to individuals in the small group. Then, in chapter seven we will discuss how to bring individuals together into a unified whole.

THE INDIVIDUAL— PAST, PRESENT, FUTURE

Each of us is unique, not only in our personalities but also in our life experiences. On the positive side, this means that each church body possesses a wealth of experience and knowledge that, if tapped, could provide wisdom, guidance and vision. A person who has experienced the death of a parent brings her own special gift to the church. Another has come from a family of entrepreneurs and possesses incredible creativity. One is from a farming family and has a special love for the outdoors. Another grew up in the poverty of the inner city and fully understands the needs that exist in our cities. Each person can bring, from experience, something that the church needs if it is to minister effectively in the world.

Yet alongside the wonderful potential there exists a great possibility for division. People from different experiences have to expend energy just to understand each other. We interpret what is said and done from our own mindset, becoming easily offended and divided.

The ideal would be an honest community in which differences could be brought out into the open, discussed and affirmed. Unfortunately, we often brush differences under the rug and misunderstand each other. Therefore, if groups are to bridge the issues that naturally divide persons, they must provide an opportunity for us to communicate in a positive manner.

To affirm each individual in a caring environment, healthy small groups will take time to share, allowing every person to tell about the unique story that comprises his or her past, present and future.

Past. We each could spend days sharing how family, friends, school, work and church have influenced our lives. We could also think back over a multitude of experiences that have altered the course of our lives. Someone's fear of heights might have come from a scary experience on a ladder. Another's stability could have come from a supportive family. One person's fear of deep relationships might have developed through a traumatic marriage. Still another person might love to invite guests over, having grown up in a bustling home with lots of guests and activity.

While getting people to talk about themselves is not the most difficult task in the world, getting them to share *meaningful* things from their past can be difficult. The major turning points of life are often crises, and some people have yet to deal positively with them. Others would like to keep a checkered past hidden from friends, spouses and children.

Your best initial questions will be easy to share, like favorite childhood memories, or the food that you have most detested all your life. People are delighted to share these, and in giving them an opportunity to share, you allow them to make a positive contribution to the group. From basic questions about one's past, then, you can move on to deeper questions, like those related to values, character shaping or pain.

Allowing people to talk about their past will help each person in the group be appreciated as a unique individual with something valuable to offer. But remember, as you encourage people to open up, no one should be forced to share; wait until people are ready.

Present. Whether a single person working a night job or a married person caring for four children while managing two jobs, each individual has present realities that determine moods, points of view, and even spiritual dynamics. We encourage one another to share about the present for three reasons.

First, leaders need to be able to better determine what each person needs. A leader might speak confidently about three-hour devotional times, while a businesswoman in the crowd dies a slow spiritual death because her business is going down the tubes and she is not able to spend much time alone with God. If you knew of her need you might soften your tone or offer to help. At the very minimum you need to know where people work, what their family situation is (children, spouse, other responsibilities), what their worship patterns are and how they feel about life in general. Understanding individual members starts with the leader and filters to the group itself.

The second reason we share the present is so that we might be a sounding board to each other's trials and challenges. Healthy groups allow members to bounce ideas off others in the group as they attempt to work out their unique life situations.

The third reason we share the present is that we better enable the group to minister to and pray for its members. We can easily make snap judgments about people when they are not present, but we tend to be far more caring when they are allowing us to participate in their lives. You cannot watch friends agonizing over particular problems without learning to identify with them in their struggles. When you identify with them, your prayers for their well-being start to take shape and a community starts to develop.

Future. Do you ever dream? If you do, what is your dream for yourself? For your family? For your church? Where do you see yourself in five years or ten years?

You may never have been encouraged to dream. Yet looking to the future is the byproduct of a biblical concept called *hope*. In the Scriptures, hope does not mean "wishful thinking," as it often does in our culture. Instead, hope is believing that God's promises will be completely fulfilled.

In the Christian faith we know a few things with certainty upon which we place our trust. The first is that Jesus will come again. We can wait for that day because we have been promised its fulfillment. The second is that we will reign eternally with God in heaven. We will

PAST, PRESENT AND FUTURE QUESTIONS

Community building begins when people are loved as individuals. Part of that is allowing people to share about themselves.

Past Questions

- What is your favorite childhood memory?
- What was Christmas like when you were a child?
- Where did you live when growing up?
- What was your greatest struggle as a teenager?
- What is your earliest recollection of God?
- What did you want to be when you grew up?
- What is the farthest place you have ever traveled to?
- Who was your favorite teacher, and why?
- How do you feel the church (in general) has helped you as a person?

Present Questions

- What is a time during the week that you can relax?
- What do you most like about your life's calling?
- What do you least like about your life's calling?
- What is one thing that gives you satisfaction?
- Which household chore would you like never to have to do again?
- What one thing would you like to change about your life? Why?
- How do you work on your relationship with Christ during the day?
- What is your greatest joy in your faith?
- What is your greatest struggle in your faith?

Future Questions

- Where would you live if you could move anywhere in the world, and why?

- How would you like to see your closest relationship develop in the next year?

- What area of your faith would you like to work on in the next few years?

- If you had three wishes, what would they be?

- If you could write one news headline for the whole world to see, what would it be?

- What is your greatest anticipation of the future?

- How do you feel God can use you in the next few years?

Using Community-Building Questions

- Learn where your group is in its group life (see chapter seven for more information); don't ask questions that the group is unprepared for.

- Don't make people share if they don't want to.

- Try to integrate the questions with what the group is doing in its study, mission, worship and so on. In this way, the questions will both build community understanding and reinforce what the community is learning.

- Ask "past" questions early in the group's life. As the group begins to feel comfortable, move to the present. As the group matures, look to the future.

one day be rid of our trials, tribulations and pains. In the presence of God there is joy and no more pain (Rev 21).

As Christians, we can wake up each day knowing that God is present in our lives and that his priorities will ultimately win out. Christians can be people of purpose and confidence, living God-centered lives filled with challenge and vision.

In small group we can encourage people to talk about their future. As they grow in discipleship, and as their confidence in God grows, they will speak increasingly of a future that is God-centered.

CREATING AN ENVIRONMENT OF SHARING

Exploring ways to allow people to share about their past, present and future is critical. Here are a few principles to guide you as you integrate sharing into your group meeting life:

• A beginning group needs to allow a leisurely amount of time for the members to hear each other's stories of the past. As members get to know one another, this sharing may decrease, replaced by a focus on the present and the future.

• A mature group needs to spend more time listening to stories about the present and the future. This sharing then shapes the group's times of prayer and healing.

• When framing questions about the past, leaders need to be especially sensitive to traumas, sensitivities and hurts that are best left protected. Ask questions that minimize assumptions (for example, that everyone had a happy childhood and two wonderful parents). Phrase questions that allow people flexibility in answering (for example, try to stay away from best/worst questions, instead asking "what is a significant . . . or one of your best . . . " kinds of questions). And allow people to share themselves without being put on the spot.

• Sharing questions are best employed when everyone receives equal time and opportunity. Many leaders model the length of time needed for answering questions by being the first to answer (the rest of the group will then tend to answer the question in twice the time taken by the leader), thus demonstrating the assumed length of time required to answer. While everyone should be encouraged to respond, people should be allowed to "pass" if they have no answer.

• The "present" question is best asked at the beginning of a meeting, when people are settling in with coffee. A simple question, "So, what's happened in your life since we last met?" can suffice. Then, the "past" questions provide great lead-ins to the Bible study. And "future" questions are great application questions, such as, "What do you think God wants to do in your life in light of . . . ?"

• Groups larger than five can easily discover that sharing time takes a great portion of group meetings. Here are two ideas to maximize sharing without harming other parts of group meeting time: First, allow as much sharing as possible to occur in groups of three or four, where people don't feel either rushed or left out; and second, try combining sharing and praying. Some groups have found that instead of first sharing prayer needs (present or future), they begin to pray and encourage members to "pray the requests," allowing God to be present and the group to hear at the same time.

• If you need to find helpful questions, the 201 Questions series by NavPress provides great ideas. Also, many Bible study guides include "past, present and future" questions.

RELATING TO INDIVIDUALS

"Hey, Sharon, I love ya!" shouts Jim, as he wraps his arm around your waist. He pulls you into a hug, asks you how you are doing and pats you on your shoulder as he waltzes away. You know better than to respond to his greeting. Jim is already reaching for the next person as he comes into contact with you. You find yourself cringing when you see him because you sense insincerity in his behavior.

How would you respond to a small group leader like Jim, who hopes that his physical touch and outgoing personality are adequate to reach each member of the group? Or what about a leader who is detached, nondemonstrative or even apathetic? How about a leader who looks down on some or all of the group members? What if your leader always has the right answer?

Here are a few principles and ideas to guide you in creating a group that does not just listen to its members but ministers to them as well.

Understand that the small group will, over time, learn to perceive individuals as you perceive them. Not only do your words and actions influence individuals, they also influence how the group will perceive its individuals. If you use guilt to get people moving, your group will learn to thrive on guilt. If you compete for glory, your group will also compete. If you are threatened by an individual, others will become threatened as well. Instead, the apostle Paul would tell you to "build others up" and "take on the mind of Christ in humility." When you minister to the individuals in a group, keep these issues in mind:

• Eye contact. When you address the group, focus on every person instead of speaking to one or two members.

• Sharing. Allow everyone to share equally.

• Cliques. Model the ability to move from person to person within the group, negating the creation of unhealthy smaller cliques.

• Sexuality. Treat members of the opposite sex sensitively, allowing healthy intimacy without either flirting with or, in the opposite extreme, ignoring the opposite sex.

• Self-Perception. The way you perceive yourself is, in a great part, responsible for how you deal with individuals. Every person in the world possesses a degree of insecurity, whether realizing it or not. But leaders need to be aware that their feelings about themselves can hinder or harm good leadership skills.

One of the greatest gifts you can give anyone is your loving prayer on their behalf. Shortly before Jesus was crucified, we are allowed an intimate look at the prayers of the Savior on our behalf (John 17:20-26). Jesus was praying for one thing—that all Christians would know the Father as he knew the Father. The cry that welled up from deep within his soul on the night before he was to die was that the intimacy he possessed as part of the Trinity would be shared by all who would call themselves his children.

This prayer should be yours as well. What is it that allows you to be a leader if not a heartfelt desire to connect people with God? The only difference between Jesus' prayer and yours is that you must also pray that you receive the same blessing of intimacy that you desire for others.

A simple idea for leaders is to place the names of every group member in a prominent place that you visit daily (refrigerator? car visor?). As you see the names, pray daily for each individual, and watch God respond to your prayers.

Develop, and place into your group covenant, three foundational rules of positive group communication.

1. Only speak about a member of the group when that member is present (the gossip rule). If gossip is present, a group will fragment; when gossip is removed, group trust grows.

2. What is spoken of in the group remains in the group (the confidentiality rule). When confidentiality is breached, great harm is done; when confidentiality is observed, individuals begin to express themselves more freely.

3. Every member, to the best of his or her ability, will be honest (the honesty rule). When people lie or mislead, an atmosphere of untruth permeates the group life; when trust is present, people grow in their faith and love for one another.

Foster interpersonal group caring. One of the most positive things that can happen in your group is that each member is genuinely cared for by the others. The leader cannot demand that the group be loving toward its members. Neither can you use guilt or manipulation. But you can facilitate the process of caring by first modeling genuine concern and then encouraging the group to follow your lead. Here are several suggestions for fostering group caring:

• Teach members to listen sensitively to one another during times of sharing (no interruptions, or side conversations).

• Encourage members to respond to what people share (within limits, as we shall discuss in chapter six). During most meetings this will involve taking time to pray for each member; on some crisis occasions, you may alter the meeting to deeply care for a person in pain, perhaps listening and praying during an entire meeting for one individual.

• Realize that the laying on of hands is not a "charismatic" thing but a biblical concept.

• Take time for fellowship during meetings to build conversational skills and group caring.

• Perhaps once every several months, take time for the group to have fun together. You may want to plan a picnic or a holiday event. These events will break the ice and encourage members to build memories, a part of group caring.

• Link the group between meetings by encouraging contact through e-mail or, for more "old-fashioned" members, telephone. This contact can involve everything from information and updates to ongoing discussions (such as on Internet bulletin boards).

• When a member misses a meeting and the group is unsure why, someone from the group should make contact. Most groups encourage members who will miss a meeting to check in and let the group know where they will be.

• Encourage (and follow) the Matthew 18:15-20 model of dealing with interpersonal conflict. When a person injures you or another, approach the person quietly, seeking reconciliation. If the person refuses to listen, take someone else as an arbiter to help you listen to each other. And if the person refuses to be reconciled, then for the good of the group, get the entire group involved and invite the unrepentant person to leave the group.

THE LEADER AND THE INDIVIDUAL

At least until the small group feels comfortable as a group, the leader will be responsible for reaching out to each individual. Two character qualities govern the relationship between leader and individual. The first is love, and the second is empowerment.

Anyone who comprehends the Bible message understands that love is one of the most important, if not the most important, concepts for human beings to grasp. In the Bible we are exhorted and commanded to love God with all of our might. We are also commanded to love one another (see 1 John or 1 Corinthians 13).

Very few people would dispute the requirement of love. However, when we get down to business, we often fall far short of really loving one another. Love requires great effort and acquired skills. It is not the warm fuzzy feeling that we identify in songs. Instead, it is an honest effort on the part of one to care for another as God would. In love, we seek the best for another person. This means that we must learn to put ourselves in other people's shoes, actively doing our best to bring them joy, and being willing to act on their behalf even when we don't feel like it. The first quality that should describe a disciple-maker is love, both for God and for others.

The leader should also empower people. To illustrate, think about the following situation: You are the leader of a group of people who will be building a shed. You are the only one who knows how to build the shed, and in fact you could easily build the shed with just one other person. But you have been given a group of twelve to help you, with no instructions on how to use the people. You have people of all shapes and sizes, ages and abilities. Now think for a minute—how would you react?

Many leaders would realistically have to say that they would end up doing most of the work while giving minimal tasks to others. This is probably the easiest and most efficient way to build the shed, and leaders are often concerned with efficiency. Unfortunately, when you do all of the important work, people feel useless. They are over-powered.

Other leaders might sit the group down and try to work through a committee structure. They could pretend to know nothing so that people could derive maximum benefit from planning and building. In this kind of leadership style, the leader would view his or her role as one of supporting individuals and overseeing disputes. The problem with this model is that very few lasting sheds have been designed and imple-mented by committees. The end product in this case might look noth-ing like a shed. When the leader does none of the work, people are left without direction.

The best way to build the shed while caring about individuals would be to take the best of the first two styles and combine them. The leader should feel very confident in exercising the maximum knowledge that he or she possesses *while* directing the individuals and empowering them to build a shed. In this instance, the leader would probably sit everyone down, share what he or she knows, and receive feedback. Then the team could break into groups, all members doing what they do best, and they could get the job done quickly and efficiently.

It is the leader's job to make things happen in a positive way. Anyone could come in and tell others how bad things are. A good leader comes in and, by reaching out to individuals, starts people moving in the right direction.

People in churches need to be empowered. The leader is going to be the one who does the empowering. Will you seek to be one who, by reaching out in love, helps people to use their gifts so that they can grow?

QUESTIONS FOR REVIEW

1. How is healthy community like a space ship, a means to a destination? What is the destination?

2. How is the idea of community demonstrated in God's Old Testament plan for Israel? In God's New Testament plan for the church?

3. In your own words, what happens in Christian community?

4. Have you ever been involved in the type of Christian community that you have described?

5. Why must we affirm each individual's uniqueness before experiencing group unity?

6. In what one way could your sharing of your past allow people to understand you better? Sharing your present? Sharing your future?

7. Using material from various places in this chapter, what are several ways that the leader can negatively impact the community? Which one(s) might be true of you?

8. What are some ways that you believe you can positively impact the community?

READING FOR REFLECTION

Here are some books that discuss biblical community: *The Safest Place on Earth* by Larry Crabb (Word), and *Community That Is Christian: A Handbook on Small Groups* by Julie Gorman and Roberta Hestenes (Baker).

IDEAS FOR COACHES/TRAINERS

Spend some time developing questions that are (a) easily answered by most people, (b) useful for gaining insight into peoples' lives, and (c) nonthreatening. Follow this structure:

• A *past* question that opens up a Bible study on prayer

• A *past* question that opens up a group study on stress

• A *present* question that enables the group to discern what is currently of concern to each member

• A *future* question that is application-oriented and based on Colossians 3:1-4

Spend some time going over your church's understanding of healthy community, and what traits it expects each small group to exhibit.

6

A CARING COMMUNITY

I can't be a part of this group anymore. I cannot handle all the tension. And I am tired of lying awake late at night after our meetings because I am so hurt. I hope you all know that I care about you, but I can't deal with this group any longer. Please understand."

You have come to the small group meeting this Tuesday evening prepared, as always, to get deep into the Bible. But your study is suddenly interrupted by Brian when he starts sharing his pain. It is as if a dam has burst, and there is nothing that can hold back the flood.

As he speaks, you want to object to what he is saying, to fix the situation quickly before it gets out of hand. But you find yourself listening intently, believing deep down that what he says is true.

You too leave the weekly meetings frustrated at times. You wonder if you talk too much, and your spouse wonders about appearing uneducated. You are able to talk to each other and calm each other's concerns. But Brian has no one to whom he can vent his frustrations. Even so, you wonder how Brian can feel as he does. He is smart, has a great personality and a good job. Why does he feel rejected and misunderstood?

Fortunately for Brian, your group reaches out in love, and his feelings are affirmed. The problems that he has addressed begin to be dealt with, and Brian feels accepted as a person. Little does he know that he has just helped your group become a more loving, accepting, caring group.

But what went wrong? Why, after months of meeting with the small group, did he feel that people were rejecting him? How could this be, when everyone wanted this group to be a place where they could find refuge?

WHAT IS LEFT TO GIVE?

Statistics, studies, reports and surveys all inform us of what we already know—our lives are fragmented, stressful and just plain hard. Many families have two working parents encountering frustration at work as well as overwhelming responsibilities at home. Children who need their parents are left to themselves because their parents are struggling to make ends meet. Singles often struggle with loneliness. Elderly people feel neglected. In short, many people are just trying to survive.

The survival mentality carries over into the church as well. People need a break, and the worship hour is often the best time they have to just relax, take a few breaths and stop thinking. This is why many church leaders become frustrated with a membership that is not engaged in active Christian living. Those members who do become involved in the work of the church tend to back away when tensions flare, because they don't want to deal with another kind of stress. Church leaders must be concerned with people who are attempting to just survive rather than to grow.

Many people in the church become overwhelmed coping with the busyness of their lives. They have enough trouble addressing the problems that come with everyday living without also focusing on spiritual, mental and emotional growth. So these needs often get put on the back burner until a day when there is enough time and energy. And that day often doesn't come.

The process of discipleship, however, involves moving people past the daily effort of surviving and into the joy of being Christ's children in the world.

SURVIVAL AND THE SMALL GROUP

Back to the problem with Brian. We can understand better why the group never recognized his pain. Everyone can be so occupied with everyday pressures that we miss the subtle relational messages that are exchanged. We are better at focusing on and understanding our own feelings than understanding those of others.

While small groups are indeed an ideal place for individuals to be cared for, we must discern the potential pitfalls. Small group leaders who want to develop a caring community need to understand how they can affect the group's perception of individuals, and how to care for those with special needs.

First we will consider the general group environment that best meets the needs of most members. Then we will consider ways that groups may minister to individuals with special needs.

HEALTHY SMALL GROUP ENVIRONMENT

"Oh, isn't he cute!" New parents beam with pride as they present the young child to the excited gaze of family and friends for the first time. Very few occurrences generate as much enthusiasm as a baby brought into a room.

We think of children as little bundles of joy, but they are also bundles of responsibility. Their physical needs require constant attention, and parents spend many stressful hours determining what particular cry communicates which need.

As they grow, children's minds need to be stimulated, so parents invest countless hours introducing them to different sights and sounds and reading them books. In addition, children need discipline to learn consideration for others.

And then come the esteem needs. Children need to be shown, in a myriad of ways, that they are loved. Without the foundation of solid love at home, the child is often handicapped in other areas of life. Rejection by parents can be worked through, but at great cost.

Further, they need to be encouraged and stimulated to grow. They might take up musical instruments or sports. Perhaps they will edit the school yearbook, or they might run for student government. A big part of growth, their spiritual growth, must be encouraged in order for them to become all that Christ wants them to be.

Adulthood presents new challenges and opportunities. Perhaps you are aware of your need for approval or stimulation. Or you may understand the importance of discipline when it comes to certain areas of your life. Of course, many adults are aware of other needs that surface because of lifestyle, such as the need for significant relationships, time off, reflection and more balance. If these needs are not addressed, we will at best stagnate, and at worst regress into negative behaviors and attitudes.

Small groups will not meet all needs. But they can address some of the most significant needs that humans possess, including biblically based needs for *inclusion, support, empowerment, and accountability.*

Accountability. Accountability involves allowing oneself to be known by another, with the result that one's actions and choices are known, discerned and challenged in light of God's truth. The author of Hebrews puts it this way: "Let us consider how we may spur one another on toward love and good deeds. Let us not give up meeting together, as some are in the habit of doing, but let us encourage one another—and all the more as you see the Day approaching" (Heb 10:24-25).

The foundation of accountability is the belief that the Bible, God's Word, reveals the true reality within which we must order our lives. People who think that realistic life is depicted in movies that glamorize greed or invite lust are mistaken. Drug use, illicit sex, and other sins are based on lies like *I'll never get hooked* or *This will make me happy* or *Now I'm really free*. Sin traps people, and being caught in a cage is not the way God intended our lives to be. Even though we acknowledge the presence of drugs, violence and sex, the greater reality, based on truth, is that people who find peace in God are truly free and happy.

People who engage in accountable relationships seek to move toward God's way of living while coming to grips with an evil world and their own life situation. What better place than a small group to discover about ourselves and God's plan for our lives?

Unfortunately, many things can hinder accountability in the small group. We aren't always honest when we deal with one another. We sweep problems under the rug, saying in effect that we don't want to rock the boat—until finally some incident causes us to take action.

For accountability to be a part of the small group, three ingredients are essential. First, *humility* must be present in both giver and receiver. We will never share weaknesses with those who we know will make fun of us later, or with those who will use shared knowledge to their advantage. We will also hesitate to address weaknesses when we know that the subject is unable to take loving correction. For humility to become an attribute of your group, the leader and individuals need to learn how to apologize, extend forgiveness, listen in a nonjudgmental manner, and care for wounded individuals.

The second ingredient is *honesty*. We are often not very honest with each other. For example, even when we are hurt we don't usually confront the person who causes our pain. When we don't, we allow people to go on hurting others or even themselves.

The small group provides a good place for the practice of caring, sensitive honesty. Some people are not ready to accept the truth, but many people are relieved that others know their weaknesses and still accept them. In this environment, people can overcome their weaknesses and grow.

The third ingredient is *self-examination*. When was the last time you went back to someone whom you might have hurt, and asked them if indeed you had done something to offend them? It's probably not something we do very often. Yet Jesus spoke about setting relationships in order when he said these words in Matthew 5:23-24: "Therefore, if you are offering your gift at the altar and there remember that your brother has something against you, leave your gift there in front of the altar. First go and be reconciled to your brother; then come and offer your gift."

Self-examination occurs when we have read Scripture together and begun to understand that it speaks to each of us. The application time of group study offers a great opportunity for the leader to ask the self-examination question: What do you think God wants to do in your life? The answer may not flow directly from the study, but it will spring out of an environment in which people are encouraged to invite God's activity in their lives.

Support. Modern life is far from carefree. We have experienced one of the greatest moments of prosperity and productivity known to humanity, yet many gains have been accompanied by a cost. One of the most significant costs is the unintentional devaluing of humans in their work. As modern corporations have sought ways to improve efficiency and productivity, many of today's workers have felt used, violated, undervalued, overworked and underappreciated.

Home life provides its own stresses. Couples struggle to develop healthy relationships while dealing with emotional baggage from earlier in their lives. Children are provided many opportunities for enrichment and easily end up too busy. Families run from activity to activity with little time together. Older adults feel like they get lost in the hectic world we have created.

A small group can address some of the life issues of its members through study. For example, many groups would benefit from a study on living balanced lives, or managing time. But a significant part of addressing stress is to encourage and build one another up so that we feel confident facing the issues that drive us. In a world where we are often told, usually covertly, that we're not quite measuring up, small groups can provide unmeasured support.

How? First, through the friendships that develop. Friendships provide intangible motivation to succeed. Second, through prayer together. When we feel prayed for, we believe that God is working in and through the prayers of others. Third, by taking specific time to exhort and encourage one another, sharing qualities that we appreciate. And finally, by simply cheering each other on.

Inclusion. We can't do better in life than to have a few close friends who know, understand and accept us. You may have heard people say something like, *We like you because* . . . and *We love you in spite of* . . . Everyone possesses certain character traits that could potentially turn others off. We guard these areas carefully, only letting people see our inner selves little by little. When we finally find a friend who loves and accepts us even when there is reason not to, there is no better feeling in the world. Unconditional love is the greatest gift one person can give another.

We come to Christ understanding that we are sinners, and we should also live with Christ's community in the same way. Small groups are effective only if people are accepted with both good and bad qualities and encouraged to try new things. When we stumble, we need loving hands, not condemning shoves. When we fail, we need approving looks, not disdainful glances. When we succeed, we need gentle encouragement, not silence. Nurturing happens when we learn to accept ourselves and each other before God.

We call the qualities of acceptance and nurture *inclusion*, as opposed to *exclusion*. An exclusive group does not just keep outsiders out; it also manifests an unaccepting attitude in many subtle ways, whether the group forms into subgroups or listens with barely concealed displeasure to a needy member as he or she shares. Nobody feels safe in an exclusive group, and that includes, ironically, the person(s) positioned by right of power and manipulation closest to the center of the group.

By contrast, an inclusive group possesses a mentality of valuing each person, whether the person is a member of the group or not. Some of the ways that a group can be inclusive:

- By intending to grow and multiply, ensuring that members consider and care about people outside the group

- By providing opportunities for the group to play and laugh together, perhaps by scheduling fun events and service projects

- By taking leisure time for sharing in groups of four, and then rotating those groups at regular intervals

- By providing, in the group covenant, the elements of positive communication (confidentiality, honesty, affirmation, no gossip) that we encouraged in our previous discussion on covenants

Empowerment. One of the qualities exhibited by healthy groups is their ability to take acquired knowledge and apply it positively. We might say that members of good groups begin to approach their family relationships in different ways; they begin to work according to a different pattern; they see the world from a new frame of reference; and so forth. They are being empowered to live the life that God calls them to.

Many people join small groups for survival reasons. But the expectation of strong groups is that every member will grow and will be able to benefit others. This means that groups need to be training grounds for people learning to better live the Christian life. Groups need to prepare people to witness for Jesus Christ in their workplaces and neighborhoods. Groups must encourage people to use their spiritual gifts to strengthen both group and church. And groups can, through multiplication, raise up new leaders who can effectively build the kingdom of Christ.

Groups can empower members to live the Christian life more effectively in many ways, including the following:

- By encouraging daily study of the Word of God, and time spent in daily prayer

- By studying resources and Scriptures with the specific mentality that the group is being trained in its faith, not just receiving information

- By encouraging members to come prepared (completed homework as agreed upon) to meetings so that they learn to provide input instead of just receiving information

- By providing leadership roles such as host or hostess, apprentice leader, prayer leader, and so forth

- By finding ways for the group to serve the church and witness to the community

HANDLING SPECIAL NEEDS

In a healthy, caring small group, people will be dropping their guards. As they do, they allow each other to see more of their struggles. We all experience insecurities and problems, and sometimes we need help. Even though peer helping is a difficult part of community building, and despite the fact that there are pitfalls when attempting to meet individual needs, *helping is necessary* because Christian love offers itself in good times as well as in bad.

Every group struggles at one time or another with special needs. Someone may be struggling with depression or the loss of a loved one. Another may be struggling with issues from childhood. A businessperson may be frustrated with work.

You should do all that you can to be prepared to minister to special needs within the group. Think back over your life in the past few years. Was there a time when you went to another person for counsel? If so, you will remember that it involved your relationship with God, others or yourself. People are relational, and we become imbalanced when any or all of these three relationships are under significant stress. Understanding this, the goal of Christian helping is to enable a person to find restoration with God, others or self.

A Christian helper recognizes God's role in the lives of people. Knowing that we are created in the image of God, we understand that true wholeness can only come through God in Christ. We might help someone through a particular crisis by focusing on the situation at hand, but we must always keep in mind that each individual needs a relationship with Jesus Christ.

Basic helping principles. Here are a few principles that may help as you deal with people in a positive manner. These principles apply whether you are engaging an individual in group or one-on-one sessions.

• *Foster responsibility.* One of the basic premises in a helping relationship is that people are responsible for their own actions. Some people do not want to walk alongside you; they want you to carry them. Your relationship with them must lead them to independence, not dependence.

• *Preserve confidentiality.* People come to you assuming that you will keep their problems in confidence. You do not have the prerogative to discuss one person with another unless you need to seek help from someone who is more qualified than you (pastor, church leader).

• *Don't promise unconditional secrecy.* On the other hand, never swear to hold everything in secrecy when someone asks for it before telling you something. As a lay helper you are not bound by law to confidentiality, and you might need to act on a rare occasion in someone's defense (in the case of suicide, for example).

• *Probe for the deeper problem.* People may come to you with what they think is the problem (or what they want you to think is the problem) when there is another, deeper issue. Make sure that you gently probe until you find the full extent of the situation.

• *Don't get in over your head.* You can do a lot as a peer helper, but some problems must be handled by professional counselors. If you feel that you are not equipped to help a person, you should say so and consult your pastor.

• *Stick with your gender.* It is wise to let men help men and women help women. There is a special kind of intimacy that occurs in many helping relationships, and sexual attraction can easily complicate matters.

• *Don't try to fix things yourself.* Many helpers are tempted to solve people's problems, especially when they perceive that the solution is very simple. But what is obvious to you may not necessarily be apparent to the one being helped. You shouldn't try to rush the process of helping just because you think you know the answers. Your job is to empower people to discover for themselves what their problems are and what they should do in response. Until they reach that point, they are not ready to deal with their problems.

• *Encourage boundaries.* An especially needy person who attempts to use a lot of group time sharing hurts and needs should be gently encouraged to be fair to other members by limiting comments to within the time constraints each person is given. If you recall from chapter five, you were encouraged to ask a question, communicate the time given to each person for the answer, and then answer the question first to ensure that the members know how much time they have to respond. This one discipline is your best defense against overly long sharing times.

• *Don't express judgments.* As you become involved in helping relationships, you will find yourself wanting to express your opinions. But sometimes your statements will come as judgments. The best way to show people their weaknesses is to ask the right questions (in a sensitive manner) or restate the problem so that they start listening to what they themselves are saying.

For instance, a man might be saying about his wife, "My wife has never even tried to love me. I don't know why I stay with her."

In response, you might say, "Don't you think you're coming down a little hard on her? My goodness, nobody is as bad as you say." But in fact that response would probably cause him to feel stronger about his original statement because you have attacked his original idea.

Instead, you should try something like this: "It sure sounds like you are mad at your wife. You are saying that she has never really loved you." This kind of statement allows the speaker to hear what he is saying, so that his next words are directed at his own statements rather than yours.

- *Avoid pat answers.* Resist the urge to say things like "You just need to pray," or "God loves you, and so do I." People need real relationships with caring friends, not preprogrammed brush-off maneuvers.
- *Pray with people.* You will find that people discover real peace when you pray with them, and this can serve as a model to help them discover restoration with God.

Crisis situations. Sometimes special situations arise that stretch you to the limits of your ability. How can you offer help when facing such events?

For example, what should you do in the case of accident, illness or death? Become involved as a friend. You need to avoid pat phrases, seeking instead to become a good listener. People who are grieving need caring, nonjudgmental people to share their grief. Small group leaders and members can come alongside as friends, helping out, listening, serving, providing tangible support.

Suicide is another problem you might face. If in the course of normal conversation someone makes an offhand comment about suicide, don't treat it lightly. No matter which situation you find yourself involved in, suicide is a very serious concern. Some people are always talking about suicide and never try it. Others "attempt" suicide, doing just enough to draw attention to themselves. Still others keep quiet and then do what it takes to terminate their lives.

When people talk about suicide, find out what caused them to mention it, and help them to understand what it is they are talking about. If you are scared for their lives, don't hesitate to act.

You do have a few tools at your disposal. You first can try to help the person as much as you can. You should also involve your pastor and any church members who have expertise in helping people. You also might want to call a local psychologist or psychiatrist for advice. In the case of a critical situation, you must involve the police. If the person is

HANDLING DIFFICULT PERSONALITIES

Your perception of individuals often becomes the way the group perceives its members. However, some personalities can provide greater challenge based on your own personality and experience. This exercise can help you to work through your feelings toward some different types of people.

1. From the list below choose three types of people who aggravate you the most. Feel free to define the types in your own terms:

- a male or female chauvinist
- a self-assured person
- a genuinely spiritual person
- an expert
- a person at peace
- a person who is always happy
- an obvious hypocrite
- a complainer
- a quiet person with a servant heart
- a racial bigot
- a selfish snob
- a self-taught theologian
- other:

2. Answer these questions for each type of person you chose:

• What makes you dislike this type of person so much?

• In what ways are you like and not like this person?

3. Imagine your small group is made up of you plus each of the personality types that you marked. List five things that you can do to work through your struggles with these personality types and encourage their growth in discipleship.

alone at home, the police can get there and stop something drastic from happening. If the person is with you, you can try to get him or her to go with you to the hospital. Most hospitals and some police stations are required by law to have trained psychologists and psychiatrists on duty twenty-four hours a day.

A CARING COMMUNITY

When things are going along as planned, we seldom take the time to think about individuals and their needs. But when a crisis takes place, we are reminded that ministry to individuals in the small group is crucial to the strength of the community. And that ministry begins with the leader.

QUESTIONS FOR REVIEW

1. In your own words, what is the main issue that is presented in the opening section, as well as the sections "What Is Left to Give?" and "Survival and the Small Group"?

2. Define each of the following needs that healthy groups meet:
   • accountability
   • support
   • inclusion
   • empowerment

3. What are specific ways that groups can ensure that they can meet the following needs:
   • accountability
   • support
   • inclusion
   • empowerment

4. How do you feel about being a *helper*?

5. Look over the Basic Helping Principles. Why are they not about trying to "fix" problems?

6. What advice would those principles offer to a group with a member who monopolizes time and energy with constant problems?

7. How could you become more prepared to be a helper?

READING FOR REFLECTION

A resource that discusses community and aspects of healthy groups is A *Different Drum: Community Making and Peace* by M. Scott Peck (Simon & Schuster).

For a book that encourages the practice of forgiveness (often at the heart of past hurts), see *Forgive and Forget: Healing the Hurts We Don't Deserve* by Lewis B. Smedes (HarperSanFranciso).

IDEAS FOR COACHES/TRAINERS

In light of the discussion in the chapter on helping people, discuss how best to handle the following situations, the specific needs of the person and how you should respond:

Situation A. Jennifer is a wonderful woman, fairly outgoing and well liked in church and community. She is a widow and has worked very hard all of her life to make ends meet. She quit school at a young age and is a little insecure around educated people. In addition, she has shied away from taking leadership roles in the church.

She recently joined a small group that you lead, and in the course of a few weeks you realize that she is not doing the work. At first you think that she lacks commitment, but when you press her (in a meeting) she begins to cry and leaves the room. You speak with her in the kitchen and discover that she is unable to read. She feels stupid. She has already decided that she must quit because she doesn't want to hold everyone back, and she doesn't want the others to look down on her.

Situation B. Jack has been in small groups in the church for many years, and somehow each group he joins eventually dies. He ends up in your small group and you quickly discover why. He has a way of imposing his own agenda on the group. He had a rough childhood, and he always seems to be going through one trauma or another that relates to his past. He has a way of "sucking the lifeblood" from people, and the group is quickly getting turned off. But when they turn away from him, the group feels guilty.

You can see that your group is going to die if you don't do something quickly. It is obvious that Jack has needs, and you believe that Jesus loves him. But what can be done to help Jack while maintaining a healthy small group?

Situation C. Charlie is a very quiet person. In fact, he is painfully shy. Even though he is married to Marilyn, a high-profile member of your church, he prefers to sit in the back of church and exit quickly. You have always wanted to reach out to him, so you invite him to your small group. He and Marilyn start coming, but he never says one word. He seems to like the group, but you are concerned because you want him to feel free to participate. Marilyn, on the other hand, speaks all the time (sometimes too much), and she answers for him. You wish that he would learn to speak for himself because you believe that he has something valuable to offer the group.

Discuss your church's policies regarding confidentiality; who leaders can approach when unsure how to handle a situation; how referrals take place when a person has a significant need; and how crisis situations are managed.

7

A DYNAMIC COMMUNITY

Have you ever worked on a complicated jigsaw puzzle? While you worked, you probably had the cover of the box with the picture of your final goal propped up as a silent but constant reminder of the end result that you hoped to attain. If you had thought about it as you surveyed the hundreds of pieces, you would have noticed that each one was uniquely cut, with its own color pattern. And each piece made sense only when placed together with the other specially shaped colored pieces. Your job as the puzzle-solver was to search for pieces that fit together. No matter how you went about putting the puzzle together, if you put in the time, you ended up with the picture that was on the box top.

Some people are better at building puzzles than others, but most people are capable. Hard work, strategy and studious concentration are all keys necessary to bring hundreds of pieces together into one scene.

In some ways, groups are like a puzzle. They involve bringing together different individuals into a cohesive whole. So the question we confront is, How do we bring together a group of three to twelve persons in such a way that their needs are met in one group? How can we "fit" unique people into a picture representing God's idea of community?

GOD'S DESIGN FOR COMMUNITY

We have billions of distinctly unique people sharing the same planet. If all of these people meet their own needs, we would have a great problem. Without unifying factors such as laws, dreams or causes to unite people, we would experience total anarchy.

Like the world, the church is a composite of millions of people. Of course, Jesus Christ is our unifying factor and the head of the church. But put twelve different Christians in the same room for a few days and you will discover the incredible diversity, and potential for conflict, that exists. Many wonder if indeed they want to be part of the same movement when they discover how different, and difficult, people can be.

What did God intend for the church? Are we just to know each other on a surface level so that we get along better? Should we get together only with those who believe, think and act as we do? Or should we unite around a particular cause, such as missions, so that we keep busy enough not to emphasize differences?

God's plan for community building in the church is that people who would not necessarily be friends in another setting come together and start the long, difficult process of becoming codisciples. Black men, White women, Indian children, businesspeople and construction workers all belong in the church. In community we learn that ours is not the only race or life situation. We also learn that we are not the only person with gifts, or sins, or trials. In short, the egocentrism that marks our existence is slowly dismantled when we confront and love people who are as special as we are.

The Bible says that even spirit beings will watch in amazement as God creates a unified church out of very different groups of people (Eph 3:6-11). It is a beautiful plan, although one full of dangers, and we have a part in fulfilling it.

SMALL GROUP DYNAMICS

Every group, like each individual it represents, has a distinctive character. However, groups also exhibit some predictable patterns of behavior and life that we call dynamics. Awareness of some of these can help you as you prepare to make disciples through small groups.

Communication patterns. You have probably seen the communication diagrams that portray what happens in the course of ordinary conversation. The *sender* speaks to a *receiver*, followed by the receiver becoming the sender. The two individuals in the diagram interpret, or decode, the messages by using their own *filters.*

Sender → ////Filter//// → Receiver

Two people might use the same phrase and mean opposite things. For example, to one person the word *home* in the phrase "I am going home" might mean a present dwelling place, while to another it might mean the place where the person grew up. Or they might say different things and mean the same thing. Each person interprets communication from personal experience.

The possibility of miscommunication highlights the importance of discovering each person's past and present so that individuals in the group can become more sensitized to what others may think and feel. A person who had grown up in an extremely strict family might cringe inside when in a conversation on the importance of discipline. Another person going through a long and painful crisis could feel guilty if the discussion centered around being joyful in the Lord. In these cases, two perfectly legitimate topics could bring very negative feelings because they are interpreted through different filters.

Whenever humans communicate, we are in danger of misunderstanding, confusion, doubt and guilt occurring. Every small group must consciously work to overcome the problems of communication if it is to become a loving community. So the leader should strive to both model and teach rules for communication. These can include but are not limited to

- encouraging people to clarify what they are saying when you are unsure

- encouraging people to be honest with each other by promoting a nonjudgmental attitude and affirming people for contributing

- sitting the group down for special communication or healing sessions when miscommunication and misunderstanding manifest themselves

Expectations. Group expectations affect group dynamics because people have ideas about the future. People in the small group have both conscious and unconscious thoughts about how the group can meet their needs as each person perceives his or her unique future. These thoughts, often unexpressed, provide the motivation for group actions.

As long as the group knows what each person expects, the group can minister to both individual and community. Problems can enter the group when people, for one reason or another, have not communicated their hopes for what the group can do for them. In this case, members might appear content when in reality they are frustrated by the group.

Every group, at every meeting, is filled with individuals who come with unspoken expectations. These expectations can be temporary, as for example when a person stays very quiet during a gathering, expecting group members to ask what's going on and show concern about something that's happened. The expectations can also be long-term, as for example when a member wants to lead the group and starts to take over in subtle ways.

You cannot stop people from desiring what they will. Indeed, you also will have your own expectations. You must make every effort, however, not to let one person's agenda destroy the group. A group with already good communication patterns will be able to deal with this problem much better than one with poor communication. A positive way to handle group expectations is to develop a clear group covenant that clarifies who the group is and what it does.

Consensus. The small group is not a democracy, where the majority rules. Neither is it a republic, where elected officials rule. Instead, decisions are made by the group for the good of the group. Each person is vital to the survival of the group; each person's opinions and feelings can and should be expressed on any relevant issue. Therefore, most decisions affecting the group should be made by consensus, which means that until everyone agrees on a particular course of action, the group waits, prays and dialogues.

The process of reaching group solidarity is difficult, but the consequences of not doing so can be devastating. The potential pitfalls of not reaching group consensus can be seen when the group must make decisions such as what new people to invite into the group, what to study, or where and when to meet. Satan works best through division. Arriving at decisions through majority rule or the will of one strong personality opens the door for problems. When consensus exists, people are affirmed and built up because their opinions are necessary. Leaders are developed through consensus.

STAGES OF COMMUNITY

A major part of group dynamics is the life stages that groups will encounter. Each small group will go through one form or another of the following four basic stages of community building. They are stage one, exploration: unity at the expense of diversity; stage two, transition: diversity at the expense of unity; stage three, action: unity alongside diversity; and stage four, multiplication or termination: affirming unity, bringing the group to an end.

Stage one, exploration: unity at the expense of diversity. Imagine that you are ready to lead your own small group. It may be your first small group or your twenty-first. You find yourself sitting with eight other people who have expressed their desire to be in a small group. Your job as their leader is to help them become the best group possible. Needless to say, everyone in that room (if they are typical) will want the small group to be a positive experience. As a result, each person will do what seems to best ensure the success of the group. The foundation for later group life is being laid, and it should be laid properly.

In the beginning, this means that people will often set aside personal feelings, small differences, and personality clashes. The unifying factor in this first stage is generally the common desire to begin a small group. So you will spend the first few weeks developing a group covenant and preparing to move forward. Then you will settle into the weekly ritual of being a small group. Like a newly married couple, you will be flushed with early successes. People may gush forth praise in these first weeks, and you may even be basking in the glow of being a good small group leader.

You should enjoy this stage, because it is the easiest. People generally lay their individuality down and are content just being a part of a group. If some are feeling tension, they keep it to themselves to avoid rocking the unified group's base. The group is free to behave

ACTIVITIES FOR BUILDING RELATIONSHIPS IN THE SMALL GROUP

- Quiet games, such as Pictionary, Scruples, Trivial Pursuit, charades and so on.

- Group discussions on topics that allow the group to know each member in a deeper way, allow each member to share something valuable, and provide a more informal and nonthreatening format within which people can open up.

- "Past, present and future" questions.

- Active games, such as volleyball, basketball or scavenger hunts.

- Group outings, such as picnics, bowling, going out for pizza and a movie, attending a concert, and so on.

- "Approach" activities, which occur before the study. These could be a question, role play, or art project that focuses the group in some way on the upcoming lesson, and gets the group doing problem solving together in a nonthreatening atmosphere.

- Meals together, whether carry-in or potluck suppers, such as for Valentine's Day.

- Parties and celebrations, such as holiday gatherings and group anniversaries and milestones.

- Service or outreach projects.

as it thinks a small group should. Unity has been earned, but at the expense of diversity. Sooner or later, diversity will make a comeback.

Stage two, transition: diversity at the expense of unity. Many groups bog down in the first stage, contenting themselves with the ease that comes with keeping relationships on a surface level. These groups often rely on a strong leader to keep them functioning. Unfortunately, discipleship does not occur when people are merely followers.

Some groups, who are willing to pay the price and who have allowed themselves to maintain open communication, will move to step two. If step one represents the honeymoon stage, then step two is the "Hey, stop squeezing the toothpaste tube in the middle!" stage. Like a newly married couple just learning some of each mate's faults, individuals in a small group will take issue with one another. Frustrations that were forgotten come back in a rush, and differences become accentuated.

People are somehow surprised when forms of conflict appear. In gearing up for the group's birth and maturity, they have forgotten their own uniqueness, as well as the distinctiveness of others. They discount or forget the great personality differences within each group of people, as well as the wide variety of personal beliefs, ranging from parenting ideas to theological issues. Add personal biases, bigotry, pride and competition, and you have a recipe for disaster!

Fortunately, a healthy small group will move into step two and begin to confront its own diversity. A group may be "going along its merry way" when one member suddenly interrupts the conversation and raises concerns or hurts. The group will often be shocked, for its unity is being called into question. Or, a group will find that several issues keep reappearing in group discussion, signaling that members are not satisfied with how the group has addressed them.

At this point it is essential that you avoid trying to fix everything to make things right again. For your group to grow, they need to go through this stage. You should be prepared to facilitate the process as well as you can, knowing that great harm, as well as great good, can come from a time like this.

First of all, you can help them realize that *everyone thinks differently*. In times of tension, people often retreat to what they know instead of opening up for compromise (or admitting they are wrong). For example, someone may offend you because he is a health enthusiast and always wants to talk about working out or eating right. If you feel bad about your eating or workout habits, you might find that you tend to disagree with him, or simply smolder with resentment. You are retreating to what you know. Healthy groups admit the differences, and acknowledge that people can learn from each other.

A second reality is that *people have different beliefs* that influence their lives. Some of these will be, in your estimation, totally incorrect. In fact, some of their beliefs will probably go against all that you have been taught about the Scriptures. One woman might not believe that a particular book of the Bible belongs in the Bible. A man preoccupied with end times might believe that Jesus is coming very soon. Someone who had a dramatic conversion might believe that everyone has to celebrate a "Christian birthday." Instead of trying to fix these beliefs quickly, admit people's differences and encourage the group to reflect on, and learn from, the ideas being presented. People are much more prone to admit they are wrong when they are approached in a positive (*let's learn what's right*) manner than a negative (*you're dead wrong and need to admit it*).

Finally, you can help the group see that *each person has a unique personality*. Your group might have a man who picks his teeth during a meeting. An abrasive woman might butt in when you need to talk to another person. Maybe a particular woman is a frustrated leader who wants everyone to be like her. Or perhaps a successful man thinks he can run the small group like he runs his company. You may ask yourself how you ever got stuck with such a group of people!

The beauty of this stage is that you are forced to recognize that people are not at all like you, even if you thought your group was homogeneous. The ugly part of this stage is that your perception of others is clouded by insecurity and fear. Like the married couple in our example, you wake up to the realization that this relationship will involve either hard work or miserable coexistence. And one of the biggest lessons you learn, if you are willing, is that it is impossible to "convert" another person. You may want to reach out and change a person who is not like you, but you will discover you are unable to change anyone but yourself.

So, you either make a commitment (as a group) to work things out until you can honestly love another, or you pretend to love, or you reject one another. If you are willing to work and make every effort to understand and love that person who is different, then you can go on to the next stage.

Stage three, action: unity alongside diversity. When you are busy trying to convince others of their faults, they pull back and deny them. But when you allow people to come as they are, they are often the first ones to let their faults be known. Your group is now entering a time when you can focus on your tasks. This doesn't mean that you forget what you have learned through the first stages, only that you apply your knowledge to build others up in Christ. You know that each new person who comes in will require some adjustments from the group. But you feel secure in the structure of community that has been constructed. In this environment, people can let down their guard and start to grow. While this stage is not clear cut or smooth, you can focus on the present and future of individuals and the group. Adding the reinforcement of periodic self-evaluation by the group will enhance your progress as a group.

By God's grace, many small groups should reach this stage and take off. If you are willing to work within this open, honest, caring environment, you can enjoy the benefits of being affirmed as an individual while discovering the unity that Christ offers.

Stage four, multiplication or termination: affirming unity, bringing the group to an end. Everything must come to an end, and small groups, no matter how healthy, are not exempt. Some groups may last a year, others ten; but ultimately, for the good of both group and individuals, the group will either multiply or dissolve at some point. A group may have grown too large, or some members have moved away. It may have outlived its original task, or some people now want to meet on a different night. A group of young couples may find that babies change their situation, while other groups will terminate each summer with the possibility of restarting in the fall.

In planning for termination, the best tool a small group has is its group covenant. If you are consistently writing covenants for specific periods of time, you can schedule regular evaluations that will enable you to determine if and how you will continue meeting. Many groups reach a point in their lives where they are not necessarily ready to disband, but at the same time they need a change. At that point they might begin meeting less frequently, perhaps once a month, to aid them as they move to termination.

Termination offers a good time for the group to look back at its history, to thank God for blessings, struggles and lessons learned, and to celebrate together. Some members will undoubtedly wish the group could quietly disband without any fanfare. However, people feel much better about a group experience if they experience an official goodbye. Plan a celebration complete with all the fixings. Look back on the past and celebrate the good things that have happened in and through your small group. This will allow your group to terminate, while providing the means by which its individuals can still look to the future.

Intimate groups preparing to multiply may develop a covenant that allows them to meet monthly for some time even after the new groups have formed. This alternative involves costly commitments of time from group members, and should be used sparingly.

ROLES AND PERSONALITIES IN THE GROUP

Think back to your high school days. Remember the different types of people and groups that existed? I remember labels like nerd, jock, brain, druggie and redneck for those who belonged to certain cliques. Labeling people, while often destructive, does give us a kind of framework within which we can understand a person's personality.

In the process of building community you will undoubtedly discover many different gifts, abilities and personalities in the body of Christ. We all function more effectively when we learn to affirm and encourage people to use their gifts for the benefit of all. Let's look at the roles, personalities and gifts people bring to the group setting.

ME-CENTERED ROLES

Do you remember in the story of Tom Sawyer when he was love-stricken with Becky? He wanted so badly to make a good impression that he generally made a fool of himself. In the process, he offended her and put his hopes for a relationship with her in serious jeopardy.

Everyone wants to make a good impression. We generally dress in a way that is appropriate to different settings, and we say things that we hope will demonstrate our intelligence, wit and charm. There is nothing wrong with trying to come across in a good way. The problem arises, however, when we use different settings solely for our advantage. There are several such "me-centered roles" that group members assume.

First, there's the *group clown*, a person whose insecurity prompts a wisecrack for everything. While this individual could bring the group together for a time, such behavior can keep the group from serious discussion and positive growth.

Then, there's the *group expert*, who makes others feel like losers.

This person does all the speaking and everyone else listens. The result is that people often feel stupid for raising questions.

A similar type is the *egocentric*, who has a bigger and better story than the one just told. Eventually this person will inhibit others from opening up.

The *one-issue individual* manages to turn every discussion into his or her one area of expertise or fascination. Group members are turned off when their own concerns are constantly twisted to fit this person's ideas.

Another type, the *counselee*, is adept at turning any small group meeting into a counseling session. Unless the group is specifically geared for counseling, and especially if this person is not trying to help herself, people either ignore this person or they are destined to listen to countless tales. Eventually some or all of the group members drop out, and the counselee has to find another group.

Although each of these characteristics hinder the group, these types often feel that they are making a positive contribution. On the other hand, much more destructive group behavior comes from the *group cynic*, who thrives on seeing bad things happen. This person loves a good scandal or failure, because it confirms his or her view of life— that it's the pits.

Another type, the *group gossip*, is always good for a few juicy tidbits about others. While expressing the desire to help others in a positive way, this person influences group perceptions about people in a negative way. Eventually the group members learn to watch their own backs around this person.

These roles all have one thing in common—they draw attention to the individual and away from others. The root problem is usually insecurity, so the leader must not only deal with the negative behavior, but also try to find more positive outlets for the people playing me-centered roles. Negative behavior must be dealt with firmly and in love if the group is to survive.

Common Roles in Small Group Settings

Me-Centered Roles	Other-Centered Roles	Group-Centered Roles
Group clown	Friend	Group-focused person
Group expert	Group affirmer	Issue clarifier
Egocentric	Group sensitizer	Question asker
One-issue individual	Servant	Problem solver
Counselee		Reality tester
Group cynic		Prayer coordinator
Group gossip		Song leader
		Mission chairperson
		Outreach coordinator
		Community builder
		Bible study leader
		Group evaluator
		Time keeper

In most cases, a gentle word of admonition will temper me-centered individuals. Sometimes the leader or another group member may speak to the person. And in extreme circumstances, such as when the person refuses to listen, the entire group may be engaged for ideas and suggestions according to the pattern of Matthew 18.

OTHER-CENTERED ROLES

Perhaps you know someone who is a fatherly or motherly type, one who can look on others with kindness, listen sensitively, and show care and compassion. These people are indispensable in the group setting, for their main ministry is to the individuals within the group. Their strength is making people feel wanted, loved and cared for, and their gift is empowering others to live life with confidence and gusto.

Included in this category is the *friend*, the person who is able to reach across race, gender and other barriers to develop a significant relationship with others. (You could also call this person a disciplemaker.) This individual often gives advice, can be counted on to listen when others don't hear what is being said, and will stand beside people when everyone else deserts them.

Another other-centered role is the *group affirmer*, a person who is adept at finding the good qualities in others and speaking about them. This person, like the one leper who out of the ten whom Jesus Christ healed returned to thank the Lord, consistently gives praise when others might miss the opportunity.

Another role is the *group sensitizer*, the individual who senses what others are thinking and feeling. A great deal of hurt is hidden during group meetings. The group sensitizer can make others aware of a member's reaction to the rest of the group.

Then there's the *servant*, who quietly moves from person to person and from situation to situation, and does the things that need to be done without fanfare. When we come into contact with a servant, we can picture the Master himself, towel around waist, teaching the disciples how they were to think and live.

The other-centered person not only meets the ministry demands of the group, but also shows the rest of the group how to care. Good leaders will not be threatened by these persons, but will recognize that they can make the group stronger.

GROUP-CENTERED ROLES

Conceptually we can look at a group as the intangible means by which people are drawn together. A key resource will be individuals who possess group-centered roles. You can find three different kinds of group-building persons. First, some individuals enable the group to understand what it *is*. Then, some will help the group to function effectively in what it *says*. And finally, others will direct the group in what it *does*.

What the group is. The basic role in this category is the *group-focus person*, who never allows the group to forget why they come together and where they are going. Because of the importance of the role, this person is a leader whether or not he or she is the official leader. Many groups wander aimlessly, some for years, with no clear direction. The group-focus person does not allow that to happen.

What the group says. Discussion is the trademark of small groups, but good problem-solving discussion is often hard to find. Some pastors and church leaders are unsure about small groups because they feel that people tend to "share their ignorance" about the Bible, which could reinforce harmful beliefs. Fortunately, the presence of some of the positive roles listed below can solve that problem.

Since groups are easily bogged down and sidetracked, the *issue clarifier* has an indispensable role in discussion. This person can remind the group what they are trying to learn and can help take a number of seemingly unrelated ideas and sum them up for the benefit of the group. From there, the *question asker* can probe by asking tough questions. A good question asker can challenge and stimulate a group with his or her inquisitive nature. Some members react positively to the question askers by posing possible solutions. The *problem solver*, like the issue clarifier, can keep the group on track. Problem solvers are often frustrated until issues are worked out. At the end of the discussion, they can bring together what was said, while the *reality tester* attempts to determine if truth has indeed been discovered.

What the group does. All of the above roles are sometimes hard to pinpoint in any one person. This is not to say that they are unimportant, for they are essential for the survival of a healthy small group. But this final category is very tangible because it involves fairly well-defined roles within the group. In fact, your group might attach special titles to some of the following people.

These functional roles can either be assigned or understood and are based on what people do best or what they believe most strongly. Groups might have a *prayer coordinator, song leader, mission chairperson, outreach coordinator, community builder, Bible study leader* or any number of other roles. It is not necessarily expected that these will be the small group leader's roles. Instead, as the leader, you become the group coordinator by placing people in areas they have expertise in and want to focus on.

Finally, two more key informal roles. First, the *group evaluator*, who can help the group obtain a realistic picture of its progress. And finally, a *time keeper* to help you stay on track time-wise.

As you can see, even a small group can function effectively as a body, with every part performing some necessary function. Most people possess more than one of these roles. As a leader, you can create an environment that encourages the more positive roles and minimizes the negative roles. Negative roles are often minimized by gentle guidance and timely rebuke. Positive roles are often simply stimulated by affirmation and permission giving.

THE LEADER AND GROUP DYNAMICS

You as the small group leader may be feeling a little overwhelmed with your responsibility. Even though we may appear to be speaking about small group ministry as if it were a scientific process, nothing could be farther from the truth. Indeed, it would be impossible to design a course that listed a step-by-step recipe for small groups. You will learn to rely on the Holy Spirit, prayer and positive implementation of leadership qualities as you put the principles in this book to work. This final section provides a framework that will enable you to ask the questions you need to answer in the course of disciple-making through small group ministry.

Good, honest evaluation will be your key to discerning how you are doing. Leaders tend to be threatened by evaluation because they might discover things that are negative. But that is the very purpose of evalu-ation—to change what is bad and emphasize what is good. We're not in ministry to be God, so we don't have to be perfect. Evaluation can show us the areas where we are weak so that, with God's help, we can become better leaders while building a strong group atmosphere. The following are a few questions that leaders should regularly ask and an-swer:

Are we as a group making disciples? We can easily lose sight of this key, primary goal of small group ministry.

Am I, the leader, an effective disciple-maker? A good leader is growing, willing to lead others in the process of discipleship, and will-ing and able to empower others to become leaders in Jesus Christ.

Where is our group presently? Develop the habit of *studying* the individuals and the group to discover where you are as a group. Unless you know the emotional, spiritual and mental state of your group and individuals, you may operate under a serious leadership handicap. A group of baby Christians might not be ready for systematic theology. A bickering group should not take in new members. When evaluating the past and present reality of the group, you will want to evaluate group strengths and weaknesses, the status, contributions and prob-lems of each individual, and the relationship of each individual to the group. If, after answering this question, you are dissatisfied or con-cerned about the group, you should strongly consider approaching the group for discussion and prayer.

Where is our group headed? Once you know where your group is, you can realistically set group objectives and start moving forward. This evaluative step is the goal-setting stage. You will want to evaluate the group both in its present state and for its future potential. Does your group want to get better at prayer? Outreach? Bible study? Interpersonal relationships?

How are we getting there? Once you have set your goals, you can move to the program. If community will be your emphasis, then you can develop a program that will stimulate sharing, fun, honesty and other aspects of community building. If you also want to study the Bible together, then you can pick a resource and move forward.

Community building is not easy, and sometimes not fun. But our churches today thirst for authentic community. The church often makes great noise about world peace, and yet we find it difficult to co-exist in a small group together. No matter where you go as a small group, you will accomplish little if you have not developed a loving, caring, honest atmosphere.

QUESTIONS FOR REVIEW

1. How can the process of community building be compared to constructing a puzzle?

2. Why do you think God wanted to bring so many different Christians together as one body?

3. Briefly state the problems inherent in group expectations.

4. How can you clarify group expectations?

5. How does working through "who we are and what we do" (pp. 135-36) define a group's identity and help the group understand its expectations?

6. Why do you think group consensus is so important?

7. In your own words, what happens in the first stage of community? second? third? fourth?

8. What situations from your past can help you see these various stages at work?

9. What different roles have you played in groups?

10. Are there any negative roles that you have taken, and if so, what?

11. What do you think are some of the most important roles to a group?

12. Why is it so important to regularly evaluate?

IDEAS FOR COACHES/TRAINERS

In this exercise (for either one-on-one or in larger groups), you will choose a leader to take you through the role play (as one of the characters), and then the leader will lead your group through the discussion questions in part two.

Part One—Support Group for Parents of Drug-Abusing Teens

You are part of a special support group for parents of teens who both use and sell drugs. You have joined the group both for support and for ideas to tackle your problem. Each of you has been under tremendous stress because of the destruction that drugs cause. You have been meeting with the other parents for a few weeks now and are ready for the next step.

For the next twenty-five minutes, your group will discuss the courses of action listed below and *will reach a group consensus* on which one of these options is best.

- Become assertive with your child. Remove all drugs and have her arrested if necessary.
- Kick your child out of the house and let him stand or fall on his own.

- Keep loving her and, if need be, allow her to use you, because you must stop being a parent and start being a friend.

- Tell him that, if he plans to stay in your house, he needs to go to counseling.

- Allow her to stay, but become more confrontational. Don't allow drugs or drug use in your home, and make her get a job.

- Put him on "probation." If he is caught by you in any wrong, kick him out of the house.

Part Two—Evaluating the Process

Spend ten minutes answering the following questions as a group:

- How did your group (if at all) reach a consensus?

- Were differences expressed? If so, how were they dealt with? (Did anyone feel put down? intimidated? If so, why?)

- Did some in the group "take over"? Did others not try to contribute at all? Why?

- Which of the roles (pp. 131-36) were present in your group?

- What did this exercise have to do with community building?

- What relational issues would this particular small group need to go through before reaching the action stage (unity alongside diversity)?

Spend time discussing your church's leadership library or resources, including small group diagnostic books and community building resources.

8

A STUDYING COMMUNITY

Cassandra had been reading through the book of Numbers in the Old Testament in her quiet time when her group made the decision to begin studying the book of Joshua together. During the third week of the study the group was discussing the end of the first chapter when they came to Joshua 1:16-17: "Then they [the Israelites] answered Joshua, 'Whatever you have commanded us we will do, and wherever you send us we will go. Just as we fully obeyed Moses, so we will obey you. Only may the LORD your God be with you as he was with Moses."

All of a sudden Cassandra sat up and began waving her hand. "Oh, oh, I can't believe this," she said. "I can't believe it took me this long to make the connection! Where is that passage I was reading this past week . . ."

A little stunned, her small group watched as she began thumbing back to the book of Numbers. Pleading for patience, she mumbled to herself, "Now, I know it was after Mt. Sinai, but before the water that came from the rock. Let's see, oh, there it is." And with that, she read to the group from portions of Numbers 13 — 14, a time when the Israelites were standing on the edge of Canaan for the first time.

Puzzled, group members asked her why she was so interested in the book of Numbers. "Don't you see?" she asked. "In Joshua 1, the Israelites are obeying God and Joshua, and they are claiming in verses 16-17 that they always obeyed God and Moses. But that's just not true. Not true at all. The book of Numbers shows that they didn't. And the last time they were at the edge of Canaan, they rebelled. Which leaves two possibilities in my mind: Either the passage in Joshua contradicts the book of Numbers, or God had changed the hearts of the Israelites in the desert."

Her observation led the group to explore two intriguing questions: First, how had God changed the Israelites' hearts in the desert (apparently without their awareness) so that they willingly obeyed? And second, in what ways do our lives demonstrate God's quiet, persistent molding and shaping of our own thoughts, attitudes and priorities?

Cassandra's group leader, Melanie, astutely allowed the group to follow Cassandra's line of questioning. Then she asked a question that opened up an exciting exploration of God's work in the group's lives: What are things you do in your everyday life that you do because God prompts or directs you? Group members responded by sharing the little things that demonstrated God's presence in their lives, such as writing notes of encouragement to colleagues who were suffering, making meals for neighbors in transition or crisis, being the only family member to care for an older parent, and much, much more. Proof that the God who led Israel out of the desert and into the Promised Land is at work today molding and shaping the lives of his children.

APPROACHING SCRIPTURE

Cassandra and her group encountered the life-changing Word of God because they spent time seeking what God has to say to us through the Word. How should you approach Scripture? The following are some general principles that provide foundational starting points for reading and study.

Principle 1. Scripture is God's complete written Word. It represents all that God wanted to communicate directly to humanity about how to live within his truth. As such, it is to be taken seriously, listened to carefully and handled prayerfully.

Principle 2. Scripture is authoritative in every area of faith and life that it addresses. We may not understand all that we read and study, but we do understand that Scripture is addressing us, and we are to listen and obey.

Principle 3. Scripture interprets Scripture. Imagine reading through Proverbs and reading a statement like, "Wisdom is . . ." You might be tempted to think you are reading a comprehensive definition of wisdom. In fact, Scripture offers many passages that in their totality define biblical wisdom. Thus, we learn to allow one Scripture to be examined in light of other passages before arriving at our conclusions.

Principle 4. Scripture unfolds the redemption story. One of the easiest Scripture-related temptations to indulge in is the temptation to make the Christian faith moralistic. For example, we read a story in the Old Testament about a "hero of the faith," and we decide that the application of the story is that we must do less of something, or more of something else. In fact, the Scripture narrative is held together by a number of concepts, and the story of God saving his people is the key interpretive motif for understanding what Scripture teaches. Therefore, every Scripture in some way either points to a need for salvation, documents the unfolding plan of salvation, provides an the opportunity for salvation or calls us to faith in Jesus Christ for our salvation.

Small groups must learn to uncover this thread if they are to embrace the one key aspect of our faith that makes us different from other religions: the grace of God. Scripture teaches that we are born with a sin nature and are unable by our own goodness to earn our way out of the problems and eternal condemnation that accompany that nature. God in his goodness and mercy has made the way of salvation contingent not upon us, but upon his son Jesus Christ. Jesus lived a perfect life, died for our sins, rose to conquer our sin and ascended into heaven to plead on our behalf. Our response: faith in Jesus Christ, fulfiller of God's plan.

THE SCRIPTURE AND SMALL GROUPS

Some people might make a case, and it carries some legitimacy, that since Scripture is so precious, we should keep its interpretation in the hands of trained leaders who can teach us all that we need to know.

Overestimating professionals. The problem with this kind of thinking is that it overestimates the role that trained professionals should play in biblical application. Pastors and church leaders are human and just as subject to error and sin as any other person. While not downplaying the pulpit and teaching ministries, we need to view them realistically. Without the balance of an educated laity, ministry can be used to lead many astray.

Underestimating the Holy Spirit. Second, this view underestimates the role of the Holy Spirit, who provides understanding and direction to the reader. The Spirit, "God with us" in the lives of believers, specializes in applying the Word to our lives. Only the Spirit can change a heart. Only the Spirit can convict a person in regard to sin. Only the Spirit can convince somebody of the wisdom of God's plan. God's Word and the Holy Spirit are inseparable. When we remove people from directly reading the Scripture, we tamper with a means that God finds effective for reaching tender hearts with his message. The Spirit will work in your life as you learn to apply principles of biblical interpretation that bring forth the clear meaning of God's Word.

Underestimating the church. And finally, this way of thinking also underestimates the body of Christ. We learn from church history that Christians are most effective when they meet together and learn from the Word of God. One of the greatest battles of the Reformation involved whether people were capable of reading the Scripture for themselves. The greatest power of the Reformation came from putting the Scripture into people's hands.

BENEFITS, SKILLS AND TOOLS

Since the study of Scripture is appropriate for a small group, we must discuss potential benefits, key skills and important tools that will best enable leaders to maximize its impact.

Each person is a teacher. Good small groups are helpful because they can bring teacher and learner roles together into one. Everyone in the small group is responsible for what happens in the small group.

Each person is accountable. Because they have a part in the learning process, all members are held accountable to complete what the group has agreed to study. If group consensus has been properly utilized, everyone will find the work reasonable and within reach. Knowing that others in the group will be expecting their participation, group members are stimulated to complete their work. Whether reading a chapter of the Scripture per day or answering questions in a workbook, they will be much more inclined to work on a consistent basis with a weekly meeting to look forward to than if they were studying alone.

Each person is challenged. Then, because they decide what they want and need to study, the topics will challenge members within the framework of their lives. Small groups can teach *orthodoxy*, encourage *orthopraxis* and embrace *orthopathy*. Orthodoxy, or right belief, means discovering what is true about God. Orthopraxis, or right action, means living a life of obedience to God's way. Orthopathy, or right feeling, means following God's will and way in pursuit of joy and peace.

You learn soon enough if people in a small group possess ownership in the group. If they come prepared and ready to share, they feel like the group is theirs. The small group leader can encourage the group to choose study materials that bring the whole group together as coteachers in the process of learning.

The Christ-centered small group will want to teach God's truth. In Scripture, people come face to face with teaching about salvation, grace, gossip, lying, bitterness, salvation, the Holy Spirit, holy living and a host of other issues. More importantly, they discover God's plan for the world and begin to find their place in history. Without an understanding of God's plan, the foundation for holy living is built on sand.

Once we understand what God wants, we are then able to act in obedience. The process of sanctification (Christian growth) involves constant enlightenment that we might live ever more by faith. The more we learn about God, the more we learn of our own failure and weakness. We are encouraged by the Holy Spirit and our brothers and sisters in Christ to work on different areas of our lives, and we grow. Although we will not attain perfection in this life, we can move closer to God's model as displayed through Jesus Christ.

STUDY OPTIONS

Groups may choose from a number of study options, including those that work you through a book or section of Scripture, and those that provide biblically based resources other than or alongside Scripture. Some examples:

- published books that cover either character or Bible book study that everyone in the group purchases and reads together (for example, *Ruth* by Charles Swindoll)

- published books that cover themes relevant to the group, such as books on prayer or parenting.

- published books, including some in the categories above, that either are or include study guides and small group questions (for example, *Managing Stress* by Serendipity Publishing)

- video training or video group resources (often including an accompanying book)

- small group materials offered by Stephen Ministry's ChristCare Publishing or Community Bible Studies (for example, entire integrated small group programs that a church or ecumenical group have purchased and intend to follow)

Of course, groups may also choose to study Scripture. With a little research, you may find published materials that allow you to pursue most of the options listed below.

Scripture memory. Joshua 1:8 says, "Do not let this Book of the Law depart from your mouth; meditate on it day and night, so that you may be careful to do everything written in it. Then you will be prosperous and successful." This verse in Joshua commands us to allow the Scripture to permeate our thought processes until we are able to think spontaneously about its truths. This happens best when we spend enough time on a portion of Scripture to memorize it.

You may make your own list of Scriptures, use a Christ-centered resource for guidance (for example, memorizing and studying the Scriptures from Handel's *Messiah*) or embrace a systematic memorization material (for example, the Navigators' "Topical Memory System") that allows a group to learn, meditate and benefit from the Scripture. The group may encourage individuals to memorize a particular Scripture, and then discuss that Scripture during meeting times.

Character study. You may locate each part of the Scripture that tells a person's story and follow that character from beginning to end. As groups study like this, they are able to "climb into the skin" of Scripture heroes. They learn that each is portrayed in graphically honest terms. Many were reluctant servants. Some were gifted speakers. All had glaring weaknesses. And God used each one to work his will in history.

You might, for instance, choose Elijah. Elijah was a fascinating person. All alone he stood up to King Ahab and Queen Jezebel with holy boldness. He faced down four hundred-plus prophets of Baal at Mount Carmel. He lived in a cave, at a widow's home and by a brook. He suffered defeat much of his life. Tracing his story throughout the pages of 1 and 2 Kings can be fun and challenging, and can point group members to a prophet in the line of Elijah, Jesus Christ, who confronted evil and won the greatest battle of all time.

One benefit of this type of study is that, although there are books that can guide the study of a particular individual, all that's really needed is a Scripture concordance, some diligence and a notebook.

Themes. Another type of study that utilizes the Scripture concordance, diligence and a notebook is the study of Scripture themes. Perhaps the group wants to learn about the person and work of the Holy Spirit. Or you might want to understand faith, or hope, or love. Your group may experience great challenge rooting out the whole Scripture teaching on a particular matter so that the group can better understand its meaning. Group results can then be checked against other resources.

Scripture study helps. Perhaps you have been involved in a neighborhood Bible study group. Or you may have used Serendipity's Mastering the Basics studies. Or you may have used InterVarsity Press's LifeGuide Bible studies. These and others like them are good Scripture study materials that have been written to help Christians study a particular book of the Scripture. They often employ the inductive approach, allowing the Scripture student to answer directed questions. People feel comfortable with these studies because the authors have designed them to allow for maximum student involvement. The group is allowed to draw its own conclusions from the study.

Inductive Bible study. Some people like to get right to the heart of Scripture study and are willing to put in the time that is necessary. For these people, inductive Bible study is a wonderful tool. Inductive study teaches you how to approach the Scripture so that you can arrive at biblical truth with confidence. Through the use of questions, and the careful analysis of each text in its context, inductive Scripture study can be the most exciting kind of study. For more information about inductive study, pick up the Inductive Study Bible or consult Kay Arthur's materials.

Book Bible study. Some groups want to study books of the Scripture without printed material and without the in-depth study that inductive Scripture study often requires. For these, studying the Scripture in the group could very simply involve each person reading a portion of Scripture and sharing what they have learned from their reading. The benefit of this type of study is that all conclusions are original and people are forced to think for themselves. A possible drawback is the potential for error that exists if passages are studied out of context.

CHARACTERISTICS OF GOOD GROUP SCRIPTURE STUDY

Leaders often fear Scripture study. The handling of the Word of God brings great responsibility, and no sincere leader wants to lead people astray. Some of this fear is legitimate, coming from a desire to be faith-

WHAT SHOULD WE STUDY?

Consider the following questions as you determine which study resources are best for your group.

- What are the perceived spiritual needs of our group?
- What options can we automatically discount?
- Which options are appealing?
- Which option(s) can help us to meet the perceived spiritual needs of our group?
- Which option(s) will provide us with the greatest challenge to Christian life?
- Where can I go to learn more about the potential option(s) that interest(s) us?

ful to the biblical text. Many ministers experience the same feeling when they are preparing to preach on Sunday mornings.

But some of the fear need not be present. People in the church are often intimidated by pastors and other "experts" who seem to know all the answers and who appear well trained. But we don't need to compare ourselves with others. God can use our attempts to do good work, just as well as those of a charismatic speaker.

Here are five disciplines that contribute to good study. If these five are present, and if the small group has the goal of discipleship, the foundation of leadership and the structure provided by community, then group study can be positive and fulfilling.

The nature of the study has been agreed on by the group. Members expect the study to meet needs in their lives. If a strong leader or a majority has pushed a study topic on the group, then some people may not feel that the study is relevant. The place to start in group study is where everyone has a legitimate, and felt, need.

The study has been broken down into legitimate units of study, and each student knows what is expected in weekly preparation. People are going to benefit from the small group study if they have work to do on their own during the week, but this can also be counterproductive. If half of the group members are setting aside times alone with God and the other half are not, then home assignments will do more damage than good. You will do better to start with small assignments and work up as people feel fulfilled in their study.

The study has definite application in the life of each group member. Not all studies will be beneficial to a group. The goal of discipleship must always be kept at the forefront of group study. A group might be fascinated by Near Eastern architecture and its theological implications, but if this course of study does not help the group become better disciples it should not be done.

The group studies Scripture in its historical context. Another characteristic of good group study is that the study utilizes exegesis (discovering the author's original intent) before attempting hermeneutics (understanding the passage in today's world). We sometimes feel tempted to make up for our Bible comprehension weaknesses by jumping to quick conclusions. But the Scripture is not trivial reading, and we are wise when we read it carefully.

The leader understands his or her role in the study process. The process of discipleship does not call for Scripture "know-it-alls," but for people who can stimulate learning and application. Small group leaders need not come prepared with extensive notes, thousands of questions or cute illustrations. Instead, the leader should come prepared to facilitate the learning process.

LEADERS' LEADERSHIP

First, the leader can *use study resources* like the ones we have talked about in this chapter. These studies can greatly aid in your preparation because you will be doing the same work as everyone else. If you understand the study's intent, you will be able to chart your own course by following and adapting that of the material.

Some leaders will woodenly follow a study, question by question, not allowing for deviation. If everyone has prepared, repeating each question could insult the intelligence of people who, having answered the questions, will want to move on to deeper levels of discussion. So the leader will want to keep discussion on course while allowing individual expression of concerns as well. A prepared group will need very little stimulation for great discussion to occur. Don't let a printed study hinder group creativity.

Second, the leader *does his or her homework before the small group study.* Most Scripture study helps are written for those who are not experts on the Scripture. Use of resources and basic preparation can help you to effectively deal with your perceived inadequacies.

Before studying a particular book of the Scripture, and to give yourself a "jump" on everybody else, read a synopsis of the book to determine author, purpose, themes, historical setting and other relevant information. Then, get a leader's guide if it is available, since this will also provide valuable tidbits. Next, work through the study carefully to ensure that you have dealt with every issue in the study. And then, when someone asks you a question and you don't know the answer, admit it. It may do the group good to wrestle with deep questions nobody knows the answers to.

Third, the leader will want to *direct the group discussion* in such a way that people feel free to express themselves within certain bounds. You don't necessarily want a discussion on prayer to turn into a conversation on how to hang drapes. You might, however, allow a person to raise her concern about why God doesn't answer yes to every prayer. If allowed, people will often chase tangents for the sake of chasing tangents. The leader could keep things on track by saying, "I'm fascinated by drape hanging as well, but I have a question on prayer that I'd like to address," or "Speaking of drapery, I have a question on prayer . . . " People appreciate a leader who keeps them moving in the right direction.

Fourth, you will want to *ask open-ended questions.* The fastest way to build roadblocks in a group is to ask yes-or-no questions. Much more exciting are questions that begin with what, where, when, how and why. So instead of asking, "Do you think this is as important as the apostle Paul seems to make it?" you will want to ask, "Why do you think the apostle Paul felt this was so important?" Good questions lead to further discussion.

Fifth, you need to *affirm each person* who speaks so that everyone's answers will be given value by others. Many people are scared to speak up, afraid that they will give a wrong answer and make fools of themselves. Imagine the pain of someone who finally does speak up and is laughed at!

Perhaps the best way to affirm people is by your paraphrasing back to them what they are saying. In this way, you are showing them that you take what they say seriously and that you are not judging them, even if you might disagree. If they are wrong, they will often discover it when hearing you recite what they have just said.

For example, someone might respond to the question, "What does the phrase 'he makes me lie down in green pastures' in Psalm 23 mean?" by answering, "I think that it refers to the necessity of sleep." You could then say, "Barbara thinks that David is talking about sleep." Even though you think Barbara is wrong, by saying this you do not judge her response. Instead, you let Barbara, and the rest of the group, hear what she is saying. As she listens to your interpretation of what she says, she may amend her response to "Actually, what I meant was that God helps us to slow down when we become compulsive, and sleep is one aspect of his care." If she does not respond, the group probably will. But in the whole conversation, Barbara must feel affirmed so that she will speak up at another time.

Sixth, use study materials and your own creative approach to Scripture study. Among the best study tools are study Bibles, concordances, Bible dictionaries, Bible handbooks and commentaries.

BREAKING OPEN A STUDY

The ideas contained in this chapter primarily involve the simple application of common sense. If practiced, the ideas, tips and disciplines will allow you to lead a positive study. Of course, if you have purchased a study guide or book, you may get ideas from those resources as well.

Here are a few more creative ideas for leaders and groups who intend to study the Scripture, either with a guide or without. These ideas take you beyond the average, ordinary small group experience and into the realm of exploration and learning.

To best experience these ideas, you may want to purchase, for the group, a concordance, Bible dictionary and Bible handbook. The idea is to enable your group to dig deeper into a text by adapting the four questions that follow. If your group purchased study guides, they will come equipped with questions to guide your group time, but one or all of these questions, sprinkled carefully throughout the existing questions, could open up your study. If you are not using a study guide, you could first read the text and discuss it, follow with these questions, and conclude by trying to arrive at the key idea or theme of the text (a modified approach to inductive study).

One further word before the questions are offered: They will only work if you come across as truly curious. In group study, some

of the best questions you frame come across like, "I was wondering
. . ." or "I'm curious about this." Curiosity doesn't kill the cat; it
unlocks the Scriptures!

*What words or phrases appear to you to be key to understanding
the text, and what do they mean in this context?* These words or
phrases might appear familiar (for example, "grace"), but by examining
them carefully in their sentences, and perhaps breaking out a concordance or Bible dictionary for further study, you could learn much
about the meaning of words and ideas.

*What thoughts, images or phrases are puzzling and must be un-
derstood if we are to understand this text?* We must, for a moment,
set aside what we think we know so that we might explore the meaning
of words and concepts. For example, in John 3 do we truly understand
what "born again" meant to Nicodemus? Exploration of that idea
might lead us to research how the Pharisee party developed, and what
they held dear; it might cause us to carefully parse Nicodemus's words
to understand his intent; it might mean that we must think about what
birth and birthright mean to a Jew; and so forth. In the end, at the very
least we will have covered some interesting ground.

*What memorable word pictures or images are located in this
text?* This is one question you could ask of almost any text in Scripture,
since Scripture is full of word pictures and images. Western Christians
can rightfully be accused of attempting to read the Bible as a how-to or
propositional work. In doing so, we often miss the color and passion
that flow, often line by line, from the authors' pens at the guiding of the
Spirit.

For example, examine these two verses for images or word pictures:
"For I am convinced that neither death nor life, neither angels nor de-
mons, neither the present nor the future, nor any powers, neither
height nor depth, nor anything else in all creation, will be able to sep-

arate us from the love of God that is in Christ Jesus our Lord" (Rom 8:38-39). I purposefully chose a very familiar set of verses to demonstrate how this question works, since we can easily imagine a group shrugging off the verses by simply saying, "God loves us very much, and nothing can take us from that love." But look again. Paul lists a significant number of items, each with visual possibilities. Why? Because he wants us to see, in our minds' eye, the very things that cannot take us from God's love!

So spend a few moments looking over the images (I see no fewer than nine specific word pictures). What would happen if your group uncovered them and discussed them in greater detail? Or if you said to the group, "I see nine images here; I'm going to read the passage slowly several times and ask you to listen for one of the images that especially grips you."

What story line do I find in this text? Since Scripture primarily uses images (above) and stories to communicate God's truth, we must learn to discern the story that is often being woven. For example, in the first chapters of Galatians, Paul presents a unique twist on his own testimony to make a point about being justified by faith. In Hebrews the author carefully weaves the Jewish history and beliefs in a clear and systematic manner while presenting Jesus as superior to everything they knew. In Malachi we confront a defeated and discouraged people of Israel in dialogue with God. And so forth.

Almost every book, including the prophets, has a story line. The story introduces you to God's chosen people (Israel in the Old Testament, Jews and Gentiles together in the New Testament) and their part in the deliberate unfolding of the redemption plan. Bible readers confront three challenges related to story line: First, where does this book of the Bible fall in the Scripture story line? Second, what is this particular book's unique story? And third, what is this particular passage's unique story? The Scripture will begin to come alive when, for example, you discover that Psalm 23 was most likely written during Absalom's rebellion when David, an old man, was fleeing for his life; or that Jesus' words in John 14 about his Father's house having many rooms were in reality the words used when a young man asked for a woman's hand in marriage.

AVOID THE PITFALLS

When you have done everything possible to prepare, the final step is to watch out for the following pitfalls that accompany group study.

- Shared ignorance, which results from a group approaching the Scripture with no clue about what it is saying to them, will lead to easy— but incorrect—answers.

- Taking verses out of context, and using them to fit your own circumstances and desires, inhibits God's Word from speaking.

- Overemphasizing certain themes which a group feels comfortable with stunts group growth. Sooner or later the group must take a more balanced approach to study and life.

- Allowing group experts to take over makes others feel inadequate.

- Focusing on only academic study, so that no application is made, and people come together for mental stimulation only, doesn't change lives.

- Using one study method repeatedly, doing the same thing year in and year out, causes groups to become bored. There are many options available, and they need to be used.

BECOME A STUDENT

Nothing will stimulate your group more than seeing its leader excited about God's Word. Like Cassandra from our opening story in this chapter, spend time in God's Word on a daily basis so that you are grounded in the Scripture. In a loving community with positive leadership, disciples will be encouraged to learn about the Scripture and apply it to their lives.

QUESTIONS FOR REVIEW

1. In your own words, why is it so important to read and apply God's Word?

2. What does it mean to study a text "in context"?

3. How are we to respond to God's Word?

4. According to John 15:9-11, what happens when we are obedient to God's commands? Why is this so?

5. What objection might some have to serious study of God's Word in small groups? In what ways is this concern valid? not valid?

6. What are some benefits that come with studying the Scripture in small groups?

7. What are the five characteristics of good group study?

8. What kinds of questions should the leader be prepared to ask?

9. How (besides looking at resource books!) could you determine an author's main purpose for writing a book of the Scripture?

10. Why is it important to get the "big picture" or purpose of a book before studying specific verses?

READING FOR REFLECTION

Kay Arthur has written materials on inductive study. Gordon Fee and Doug Stuart have written the bestseller *How to Read the Bible for All Its Worth*. Some effective Bible resources (besides some mentioned in this chapter): *New Bible Dictionary* (InterVarsity Press);

Eerdmans's or Unger's Bible handbooks; concordances like Cruden's or Strong's; and for a commentary series that gives historical background on texts, the *IVP Bible Background Commentary* series is very helpful.

IDEAS FOR COACHES/TRAINERS

Create a Bible study. You will need both a leader and a fairly organized secretary. In this session you will create a Bible study on Luke 16:19-31.

Step 1: Read the text. Attempt to arrive at a consensus on the main point of the passage. Write that point down. This purpose statement will be your objective throughout the study.

Step 2: Develop an "approach," or community-building, activity connected to the purpose. This question, or set of questions, will allow small group members to relax while preparing for the study. For example, if the main point of the passage is service, you might ask individuals to relate experiences with waiters and waitresses in restaurants. This will allow you to zero in on the topic while having fun at the same time. If you need help thinking about this question, you might review chapter five when we discuss the *past, present and future* questions.

Step 3: Create a set of questions that will draw people into answering the four probing questions offered in this chapter.

Step 4: Develop a question or two that will help the group make modern application of what they learned.

9

A WORSHIPING COMMUNITY

Picture sixty thousand fans, packed into the colossal Skydome, watching the baseball game of the century. Two of the best teams in recent memory are locked in mortal combat, both attempting to ensure their place in baseball history. Tension is written across all of the players' faces as they give every ounce of their energy to winning. The game has wound down to the seventh game of the World Series. Each team has won three games, and now the teams are tied entering the bottom of the ninth inning.

The home team is at bat, the best reliever in the league on the mound for the visiting team. First one out, and then two, and the hopes of the team rest upon the shoulders of Harv Iceberg, the incredible home-run slugging outfielder. He waits for the right pitch, sending a few into the foul zone and working the count to three and two. All the fans are on their feet. Each time the pitcher looks to the catcher for the sign, the crescendo builds in a steady beat until the sound rocks the very foundations of the stadium. Then, as the pitcher goes into his full-count wind-up, the noise becomes deafening.

And then it happens. Almost as if it were written into a script, Harv sends the three-and-two pitch high into the upper deck of the outfield. He is immediately swarmed by fans and teammates, while those in the stands clap, cheer and raise their hands to this man who won the game. The revelry will continue long into the night as the stadium empties and excited fans pour into the streets of the city.

Now try to picture this: There is a hush in the auditorium as the ballet performance nears its end. For two hours the audience has been given the treat of watching some of the best ballet dancers in the world, and each has seemingly outdone himself or herself in this performance. There is one dancer, however, who has emerged to stand above the others. A young, unheralded dancer has touched the hearts of each person with her sensitive, artistically flawless performance.

In this, the final scene, she is dancing the final steps to the ballet. As she finishes, flushed and dainty, the crowd erupts in thunderous applause. Every heart in the auditorium is warmed, not just by her performance, but by their own response to her. As she curtsies to the crowd, people bring roses to show their enthusiasm.

And finally, picture this: The mob in front of the posh Grand Hotel is stifling under a blazing sun. Some people have been there since before dawn. Word has somehow leaked out that Flash Jenkins, the rock star of the decade, is to arrive sometime early in the afternoon. Young girls, middle-aged men and even older women are crammed together in the hope that they will somehow glimpse this modern-day hero.

Finally a stretch limousine pulls up, and Flash, surrounded by bodyguards and local police, emerges onto the sidewalk. The crowd shouts in glee and presses upon the small entourage as they struggle up the sidewalk to the hotel. Some people actually get through and touch his clothes, while others have to be content with a close-up look at his face. When Flash, in a rare moment of generosity, stops to autograph a young girl's album, others in the mob scream as they picture how they would feel if he stopped to touch their own album. With voices and hands raised, they shout praises to this rock prince.

Three scenarios; one common element. Have you detected it? In each story, one person has captured the hearts of people and received praise and glory for an accomplishment. And while you might not personally act the same as the audience in any of these examples, the point is that praise, or worship, comes naturally to humans. We praise good speakers, great athletes, wonderful singers and musicians, and a host of others who are gifted.

TYPICAL CHILDREN

We enjoy worship, it is true. But heartfelt worship for God doesn't come easily to many people. To discover why this is so, consider the example of children relating to their parents.

The typical child makes many demands of his or her parents, in fact often pushing them to the limit of their giving capabilities. Infant cries for love and care are replaced by "Ga ga goo" (or, "Give me my bottle!"). Toddler demands are replaced by "Daddy, can I have some money for an ice cream cone?" Childhood demands are followed by "Mom, I'm going to the movies with friends, and I need $10 and the car."

Imagine the relief that comes to parents of children who, upon reaching adulthood, choose to become friends with their parents. A child-friend is able to move past the arena of personal need into a genuine relationship with his or her parents.

Now think of how the typical Christian approaches God, our heavenly Father. Like the baby, or the child, or the adolescent, we generally approach God with "Dear God, I pray that . . ." We tend to come with our shopping list of requests as if he were the cosmic father whose main purpose in life is to cater to our needs and the needs of others. In doing so, we miss a vital part of our relationship with God.

A rare child takes time to genuinely express love or thanks. But when it happens, the parent's heart is blessed and the gratitude strengthens the bond between parent and child. This, on an earthly level, parallels our experience in worship with God.

When we approach God with genuine praise and thanksgiving, we experience a wonderful closeness to our Father. It is almost as if we climb into his lap, rest our head against his chest and tell him how safe we feel when his strong arms are wrapped around us. Most children take their parents' love for granted. We too take God's care for granted.

REASONS WORSHIP IS IMPORTANT

Here are six reasons worship is essential.

God is worthy of our worship. We worship God because the things we say about him are true. He is faithful, loving, powerful and kind. He offers salvation through Christ, and he enters the life of the believer. When we begin to grasp the truth of God, praise, thanksgiving and offering begin to well up in our hearts, for we have touched the greatness of our God.

We experience joy in worship. If someone is a great figure skater, we don't compliment that person on his or her basketball ability. We speak truth when we affirm his or her skating abilities. We do the same with God, and when we do so, joy begins to well up in our hearts. To truly worship God, to be in his presence, is to know joy.

Worship is essential to life. We spend our lives searching for what will bring the greatest satisfaction, and when we think we have found it, we give our all to it. Christians struggle because we, like the rest of the world, are led to believe that material possessions, or power, or other worldly offerings, can give happiness in life. But over time, through worship, we realize that there is joy and peace only through living in God's will. By focusing our lives on God, we are able to bring relationships, thoughts and actions, and lay them at God's feet as our spiritual offering. As we do this, we fulfill our natural earthly desire for worship. You've got to worship someone (or thing)—it might as well be God!

We are practicing for heaven. In Scripture, whenever the curtain that hides our view of heaven has been pulled back a little, it always reveals one action in progress. Worship. Revelation 4:8-11 gives this snapshot of heaven:

> Each of the four living creatures had six wings and was covered with eyes all around, even under his wings. Day and night they never stop saying: "Holy, holy, holy is the Lord God Almighty, who was, and is, and is to come." Whenever the living creatures give glory, honor and thanks to him who sits on the throne and who lives for ever and ever, the twenty-four elders fall down before him who sits on the throne, and worship him who lives for ever and ever. They lay their crowns before the throne and say: "You are worthy, our Lord and God, to receive glory and honor and power, for you created all things, and by your will they were created and have their being."

Just imagine, night and day, without fail, they sing the praises of their God! In heaven, when all of the smoke of life has been cleared away, we will comprehend that the ultimate and only reality is God. So why not try to learn this now, by focusing our lives on worshiping God?

We sin when we don't worship. If we were indeed created to worship God, then we sin when we ignore our calling. In fact, Romans 1:21-23 connects a lack of worship with immorality:

> For although they knew God, they neither glorified him as God nor gave thanks to him, but their thinking became futile and their foolish hearts were darkened. Although they claimed to be wise, they became fools and exchanged the glory of the immortal God for images made to look like mortal man and birds and animals and reptiles.

Notice in this passage that they neither praised God nor thanked God, the first two elements of worship that we talked about. The result was that they found it easy to ignore God and turn to lives of sin.

When we forget to worship God, we begin to lose connection with who and what are important in the world—who provides and cares for us, and what he expects from us. Our focus becomes me-centered, as opposed to God-centered. When we don't worship, we sin.

The devil hates when we worship God. As long as we are me-centered, the devil does not have to listen to us adore and praise God. But when we become God-centered, the devil cringes because our praise, thanks and very lives become focused and meaningful. His role is to sidetrack and frustrate, while God is there to give meaning and joy.

WORSHIP IN THE SMALL GROUP

In the small group, disciples are getting to know God better. As God starts to touch lives, and as God's children learn to respond in praise and thanksgiving, and by offering their lives, then worship becomes a necessity. Worship belongs in the small group.

Many groups, however, struggle to find an appropriate place for worship. And, when they attempt to worship, they discover that long, unfocused sharing times and other group activities steal worship time. Significant numbers of groups give up on worship entirely.

Here are some practical suggestions that may enable your group to experience more, and better, times of worship:

• Worship is not meant to be a separate or distinct kind of activity; instead it should underlie all that you do. If your group can cultivate an awareness of what God is doing and a subsequent awe for his greatness and love, then your times of study, prayer and fellowship will be enhanced. For example, during a study time you may simply introduce the question, *What do you see in this passage about God?* Allow the members to explore who God is and what God is doing, and to express admiration to and for him.

• Without fear of contradiction, while worship should underlie all we do it must also be introduced as a separate discipline so that we may learn what worship is, and how to worship. This time may be rotated within group meetings, although many groups that worship are blessed by having a separate time right before engaging in study (as a way of preparation), or before/during/in place of a sharing and prayer time.

• If you employ a distinct time of worship, be creative. Use the gifts present in the group—for example, those with musical backgrounds for singing or instrumental support. Enjoy different modes of worship, such as those involving singing, listening, speaking, creative reading, poetry, praying and more. Bring in outside means of worship, such as sing-along tapes, songs by Christian artists, books of poetry and so on.

PURPOSE OF WORSHIP

In worship we begin to learn who God is and what God does. Our knowledge builds trust in God, enabling us to be better equipped to live a balanced life. A deeper relationship with God brings a sense of closeness and security that carries over into other areas of our life (including prayer). Like the child who has come to appreciate her parents and has stopped using her parents for her own good, we can start working *with* God instead of "working God." Worship is a special kind of key, for it unlocks many doors to deeper Christian joy.

So what is the purpose of worship? To declare, through praise, thanksgiving, and our very lives, the worth-ship (or worthiness) of God, as we lift our hearts in love and reverence to God.

If you recall the earliest pages in Genesis, human beings had started giving sacrificial offerings to God as an expression of their devotion. Even though sin had marred the human and divine relationship, humanity attempted to worship God by bringing things to him that were very important to them. And in its very essence, worship does involve bringing an offering, our offering, to God. Coming from imperfect humans, all that we offer is sin-stained and imperfect. Yet, we are the ones who benefit when we worship God.

We may practice three basic components, or "offerings," in Christ-centered worship. In worship we *praise*, then we *give thanks*, and finally we *offer our lives* to God.

PRAISE

Perhaps without realizing it, we expend great energy searching for things that bring joy, satisfaction and fulfillment. The hiker will look with excitement to each new summit. The expecting parents will marvel at each young child that they see. The young dancer will watch enthralled as an expert dancer performs intricate maneuvers.

This desire for meaning is present in humans because sin created a vacuum where close fellowship with God had previously existed. In the Garden of Eden, Adam and Eve enjoyed a special closeness with God that was based upon genuine, uninterrupted adoration of God. Then Satan entered the picture in Genesis 3 by appearing to offer Adam and Eve the same place, and therefore devotion, that God alone inhabited. In response, they turned from worshiping God so that they too might be worshiped. Successive generations have proven that human goals—searching for riches, power and fame—are driven by our need to be the center of worship and to be in control. For those who can never attain power or control, there is disillusionment, frustration and bitterness with life.

Some, however, have found peace because they have discovered at least a partial restoration of the Genesis relationship. These few have looked past themselves and their own small worlds and have come to know One far greater who is worthy of their praise. They have found joy by trading in their self-centered lives for God-centered worship.

Christian praise focuses on who God is and what God does in and among his creation. When we praise God, we attempt to think about his nature and actions and to respond in faith and adoration. In order to enhance your understanding of praise, read Psalm 145 and underline every reference to who God is and what God does in creation. Then meditate on what each one means.

If you examine this and other psalms of praise closely, you will notice three emotions that naturally flow from what we learn about God.

I will exalt you, my God the King;
   I will praise your name for ever and ever.
Every day I will praise you
   and extol your name for ever and ever.

Great is the LORD and most worthy of praise;
   his greatness no one can fathom.
One generation will commend your works to another;
   they will tell of your mighty acts.
They will speak of the glorious splendor of your majesty,
   and I will meditate on your wonderful works.
They will tell of the power of your awesome works,
   and I will proclaim your great deeds.
They will celebrate your abundant goodness
   and joyfully sing of your righteousness.

The LORD is gracious and compassionate,
   slow to anger and rich in love.
The LORD is good to all;
   he has compassion on all he has made. . . .
Your kingdom is an everlasting kingdom,
   and your dominion endures through all generations.

The LORD is faithful to all his promises
   and loving toward all he has made.
The LORD upholds all those who fall
   and lifts up all who are bowed down.
The eyes of all look to you,
   and you give them their food at the proper time.
You open your hand
   and satisfy the desires of every living thing.

The LORD is righteous in all his ways
   and loving toward all he has made. . . .
My mouth will speak in praise of the LORD.
   Let every creature praise his holy name
   for ever and ever. (Ps 145:1-9, 13-17, 21)

First, we experience *anticipation*. The psalmist appears to be excited about what he is learning, and will learn, about God. In this psalm, the author promises that he will exalt God, will praise him, will tell of his mighty acts, will meditate on his wonderful works. Rather than ending, one positive time of worship will lead to others as we anticipate yet another wonderful time with God.

The second emotion expressed is *appreciation*. Like a starving man savoring every bit of a gourmet meal, the psalmist examines, with obvious pleasure, a great many attributes and activities that define who God is and that God does. The psalmist apparently enjoyed writing this love song to God. He knew, as we also know, that you cannot worship God without appreciating and experiencing God.

The third emotion found in the psalm is *awe*. If you were to meet your favorite actress or sports hero, you might approach that person with a measure of awe. So also on a much grander scale we learn to respond in awe to a powerful, creative, loving, gentle, compassionate God as we learn more about him.

These principles may sound great, but praise is a very difficult concept to grasp and apply in life. Many people struggle to offer praise to One who is not physically present. How can we get excited about someone we cannot see? God has provided help for sincere believers.

First, *Christians have the Holy Spirit in their lives*. The Spirit helps us worship God, and we can find comfort in the fact that weak, fumbling efforts are being directed by the Spirit. Second, *worshiping God is a discipline*. Even though worship comes naturally, worshiping God is something that we have to teach ourselves over a lifetime of loving God. We will naturally expend much effort reorienting our thoughts from self-centered obsession to God-centered devotion. Third, *we have a wonderful resource in the plethora of God-centered praise in Scripture.* By meditating on these passages, we can learn how to lift our hearts before God in praise. Fourth, *we can find things to praise God for by examining creation*—even little things in nature, like delicate flowers. We can praise him for his creativity in designing the flower. And we can praise him for his knowledge, because he knows each particular flower (in fact, according to Matthew 6, he adorns them!). Finally, *we have each other.* When we come together and share God's greatness and goodness together, we are greatly blessed.

If you want to experience praise with your small group, you might bring a flip chart or white board to your group and brainstorm ways your group can praise God. Once you have a list of possibilities, whittle it down so that you participate in those that are most practical based on your group's gifts and abilities. The possibilities for worship are endless. We will never be able, in a small group resource, to list the many opportunities and small nuances that could bring exciting worship into your group. Here are a few key ways to introduce praise:

• Use psalms. The book of Psalms is a compiled list of songs that take the form of praise and thanksgiving hymns as well as prayers. In the psalms we come into contact with people who attempted to worship God in all the varied circumstances of life. The psalms include themes ranging from war to creation, bitterness to joy, fear and frustration to victory and celebration. When reading Psalms, we can identify with the psalmists and their varied human experiences. Even when they were expressing terrible fear or struggle, they almost always ended the psalm by expressing their confidence in or devotion to God. In doing so, they gave us a model for dealing with life. In the small group, you may want to have a worship time in which people share their favorite psalms, or you may open prayer time with the reading of a psalm. Reading and discussing the psalms will reinforce a deeper love for God in the group.

• Ask group members to share a favorite Scripture that tells something about who God is and what God does. Let them explain why they love the Scripture.

• Incorporate hymns. Some of the people in your group will have grown up singing hymns. Some of the good old hymns can provide a wonderful worship experience in the small group. Colossians 3:16 talks about singing "psalms, hymns and spiritual songs with gratitude in your hearts to God." Hymns represent a more traditional praise approach, because they generally focus on praise for who God is and what God has done. If your group has a pianist, you can have great fun singing hymns to accompaniment. If not, you may sing a cappella or simply read favorite hymns.

• Incorporate praise songs. Praise songs are generally more experiential (what God has done for me, the focus of thanksgiving), but some speak about who God is and what God has done. These songs may be read or sung.

• Offer a prayer time in which your prayers simply affirm God in praise.

• Have a group member read a portion of Scripture that reveals who God is in some way, while the other members close their eyes and listen. Reread the passage, and have members share what they heard about God.

• Include liturgy. Perhaps in reaction to the widespread use of experiential praise music, many people are gravitating toward the majestic, mystical and liturgical aspects of worship. Groups may find that liturgical resources like the Book of Common Prayer provide rich forms for worship as well as prayers. You may also tap into meditative and contemplative prayers (for example, of Henri Nouwen) and mystical or contemplative singing (Taize).

THANKSGIVING

The focus in thanksgiving is on what God does on our behalf. Thanksgiving takes the God-centered perspective in praise and applies it to our individual lives. In giving thanks, we realize that God, who is at work in the world, is also present in every area of life itself.

Thanksgiving is important because we easily forget where blessings come from. The great church response, the Doxology (meaning "Praise God"), contains these words: "Praise God, from whom all blessings flow!" A genuinely thankful person remembers that an exclamation point follows "flow." We are sure to be happy when we thank God!

Just as with praise, we find it difficult to give thanks. Yet God has given us much to thank him for. With humble gratitude in our hearts, we remember how Jesus suffered so that we could know God personally. With growing joy, we can sense the Spirit at work in our lives and thank God that we have been given the Spirit "who is a deposit guaranteeing our inheritance" (Eph 1:14). As we look forward to heaven, we thank God that we have a reason for living.

We can also thank God for each healthy day we enjoy, for each breath we take, for each day with family and friends. We can be grateful that God has called us to be his servants. Additionally, we can thank God for all of the material blessings that we enjoy (often without realizing their benefit until we don't have them). And we can even thank God for our suffering because, as Peter says, "These have come so that your faith—of greater worth than gold, which perishes even though refined by fire—may be proved genuine" (1 Pet 1:7).

Thankfulness always starts with a desire to give God the credit for his goodness, and that requires concentrated effort on our part. Eventually, though, we reach the point where both praise and thanksgiving pour forth from grateful hearts.

• Offer a time of thanksgiving, perhaps in the context of a sharing time, in which people offer thanks for what God is doing in their lives.

• Have a member of the group keep a prayer journal of all requests being made during the year. Sometime during the year, or perhaps several times, revisit that journal to see the answers that God has provided. Give thanks for what God is doing and has done.

• Ask members to share a time in their lives when they suffered, and yet experienced God's presence and love in deeper ways. One of the great realities of the Christian life is that God can turn our hurts and defeats into victories.

• Colossians 3:16 mentions "spiritual songs," or as they are known in modern church life, praise songs, probably because they represent a more experiential aspect of the Christian faith. Where hymns tend to be doctrinal, praise songs often represent our perception of what God is doing in our lives (thanksgiving). These songs are generally simple. They easily adapt to guitars or sing-along albums, and they have varied rhythms and beat. You may sing the songs, ask people to share their favorite song (perhaps a favorite CD or tape?), or simply read them.

• Most worship involves talking *about* God. In prayer, you can also worship by talking *to* God. When we worship God in prayer, we use the highest form of communication (prayer) for our highest action (worship). What better combination is there? Ask members to pray to God, giving thanks to him for whatever is on their hearts.

• Sometimes we can both worship and learn when we read prayers in the Bible (including the psalms), because they provide a good model for those who would worship God in prayer. These prayers generally contain a number of references to what God has done in the life of the one praying. Even in prayers in which people are making requests, praise and thanksgiving are almost always present. By telling God he is great, we become more confident in his ability to guide our lives.

OFFERING OUR LIVES

Praise and thanksgiving are only the warm-up for true worship. For, as is stated again and again in the Scriptures (see Ps 51:16-17), God doesn't want our offerings if we are somehow detached from them. God wants us. Romans 12:1 says it this way: "Therefore, I urge you, brothers, in view of God's mercy, to offer your bodies as living sacrifices, holy and pleasing to God—this is your spiritual act of worship." When we offer ourselves to God, we are performing a spiritual act of worship.

With this third element of worship, we begin to understand the nature of worship. Worship is a personal expression, a deeply rooted response. To worship lightly would be like going to a football game and pretending to be a great fan, without knowing the rules or caring about what happens. For us to worship, we must actively engage our heads, our hearts and our very lives in knowing and serving God. For the fact remains that the greatest offering we can bring to God is ourselves.

How can a group and its members bring themselves as an offering into worship? Perhaps by offering a special "service of consecration" at regular intervals, in which people share what God has done in their lives and they commit to asking God to continue that work. On a weekly basis, the application time of study provides an opportunity for members to commit themselves to walking closely with God as God changes lives.

GETTING STARTED

You can imagine, even with what you have learned in this chapter, the difficulties inherent in teaching a group to worship God. Worship calls forth deep feelings, and wherever there are deep feelings, there will be some discomfort.

A few simple steps will help you introduce worship in a more non-threatening way. First, *be willing to start with yourself.* Use the worship ideas above to explore ways that you can be more worshipful in your personal life. The best creative worship ideas will come from you as you learn how to worship God.

Second, *be willing to go slowly.* Start with a song or two, or the reading of a psalm. Over time, and with your good leadership, the group will relax and want to spend more time worshiping. Then you can learn to use the different gifts that you can find in the group. If some have special musical ability, use their talent to enhance worship through song. If someone loves the psalms, or loves to share about God, let him or her lead parts of the group worship time. A grass-roots worship movement can be very inspiring. Let the people help each other worship God.

Finally, *keep worship fresh and creative.* When people get used to something, they often stop thinking about what they are doing. If you sing the same songs week in and week out, you will stagnate. On the other hand, by tapping into your group's creativity you may employ many exciting worship ideas. You can memorize Bible verses, have worship-oriented skits or use rhythm instruments to lighten the atmosphere. Weave ancient, traditional, liturgical, intimate, spontaneous and modern elements of worship to enhance the experience. Allow worship to be an expression of your own dynamic relationship with, and love for, God.

COMMITTING TO WORSHIP

Is it your hope that you and your group will fall in love with Jesus in

WORSHIP IDEAS

These ideas will help you to lead the group in nonthreatening, creative worship activities:

Scripture

• Read psalms before prayer time.

• Memorize praise portions of Scripture.

Song

• Make use of instrumental or song-leading gifts.

• Sing hymns.

• Sing Scripture songs.

• Sing favorite praise songs.

• Use tapes, records and albums by professional musicians.

Sharing

• Spend part of group time expressing thanks to God.

• Spend sharing time discussing what you are learning about God's nature and activity in the world.

• Discuss ways that you as individuals and a group can learn to worship God.

Prayer

• Allow a moment of silence before prayer time to encourage people to "get in tune" with God.

• Encourage people to thank God in direct proportion to each request prayed (for example, if a person makes one request, they should also give at least one item of thanks).

• Set some prayer times aside for the sole purpose of worshiping God.

a deeper way? Do you think worship will help you in your quest? If so, then commit yourself to a life of worship. Your own declaration of God's worth-ship will go a long way toward focusing your group in worship.

QUESTIONS FOR REVIEW

1. How do the illustrations in the first section demonstrate our natural desire for worship?

2. How would you define the purpose of worship in your own words?

3. What are the three basic components of Christ-centered worship?

4. How would you describe each of the three components?

5. What are some of the specific ideas for group worship that you feel might be most helpful in your experience?

6. What do you feel are some of the potential pitfalls to group worship?

7. What are ways that you can introduce worship into the small group experience?

8. How will your life of worship enable the group you lead to respond to God?

READING FOR REFLECTION

Most Christian bookstores or publishing houses have separate sections listing worship resources. You have many to choose from, including hymn books (Word, Gaither, denominational), praise books (Maranatha, Integrity/Hosanna, Vineyard), books of poetry and prayers, and books about worship.

IDEAS FOR COACHES/TRAINERS

For each of the three categories (praise, thanksgiving, offering self), devise an actual worship experience to be used in groups.

Visit your church's library, or a local Christian bookstore, to locate resource books on worship.

10

A PRAYING COMMUNITY

You are trapped, and you know it. There appears to be no way out, at least no easy way. You must simply attempt to make the best of a bad situation.

You had come to church to let go, to worship, to find refreshment and stimulation. Instead, you find yourself pinned in a corner of the fellowship hall listening to the ramblings of a very needy individual. If only this person would catch his breath, you might find a way to leave. But he somehow maintains his stamina while connecting an endless series of run-on sentences.

After a while you go numb. His face has doubled in size. His hair becomes a forest, and you imagine yourself lost among its foliage. His nostrils flare, and you recoil at fire that seems to be coming out. Then, when he laughs and punches your arm, you are brought back to reality with a jolt. How will you ever remove yourself from this predicament? Will your youngest child remember you when, and if, you finally get to go home?

Eventually, and with tremendous feelings of guilt, you extract yourself with a mumbled excuse and a hasty retreat. He follows you for a while, then gives up and heads for another person. As you hurriedly exit the hall, you remind yourself to take drastic measures the next time you see him coming. If you see a tree handy, you will jump into its welcome branches. If you can reach a chandelier, you will swing to freedom. No matter what, you will get away!

This person frustrates you because he is unable to communicate. He can talk, and he thinks that he has much to say, but in fact meaningful dialogue with him is minimal, because he cannot listen. And this is where your difficulty lies. You cannot connect with this person because he will never understand you. He has used up all his time and energy on himself. You want to help this person, but as a realist you understand that you will probably get nothing in return.

God created us to be relational creatures. We need to be understood, and we also need to understand. Relationship occurs when two persons meet, reach out and love one another. In understanding, we are understood. In loving, we are loved.

This principle of reaching out in relationship—communication—undergirds our understanding of prayer. In prayer we seek to be known (by God). In prayer we also seek to be knowing (of God).

If we are not involved with God in relationship, we will miss much that the Christian life has to offer. And every relationship starts and ends with communication.

POOR IN SPIRIT

When prayer is mentioned, many images, feelings or perceptions probably come to mind. You may think of the various parts of prayer, like confession or worship. Then again, you might focus on theological truths, such as God's power and love.

On another level, personal feelings also reveal a great deal about what we think of prayer. All praying people struggle with insecurity and guilt about their prayer life. Many people feel that they don't pray enough. Others feel inadequate because of sin or low self-image. Still others wonder if anyone listens, for they do not feel heard and valued in life.

Perhaps intimidated by super-religious people, or maybe without a good Christian role model, many individuals feel completely overpowered when it comes to living a life of prayer. They say, in essence, "We don't know God, and we have no idea how to get to know him."

Insecurity comes out in small groups as well. Most people, even those willing to try, are intimidated by group prayer. Because of this, prayer times may be characterized by silence and tentativeness instead of boldness and joy.

If you can connect the parallels, we may seem to be like the man in the story at the beginning of this chapter. We bring many deficiencies and needs to our relationships with God, and we appear to offer nothing in return. Do we appear, to God, as the man who drones endlessly and really says nothing?

No. We part ways with our needy friend when *we care* how God is responding to us. In trying to understand God, we are making an honest effort at communication. The tension that results from our insecurities may come from a desire to be close to God in a healthy way. We must learn to address insecurities, and this chapter can help, but the presence of tension can be a healthy sign that we are reaching out and trying to know God better.

PHARISEE OR SINNER?

In Luke 18:9-14, Jesus tells a story that sheds light on what our attitude can be when approaching God in prayer:

> To some who were confident of their own righteousness and looked down on everybody else, Jesus told this parable: "Two

men went up to the temple to pray, one a Pharisee and the other a tax collector. The Pharisee stood up and prayed about himself: 'God, I thank you that I am not like other men — robbers, evildoers, adulterers — or even like this tax collector. I fast twice a week and give a tenth of all I get.'

"But the tax collector stood at a distance. He would not even look up to heaven, but beat his breast and said, 'God, have mercy on me, a sinner.'

"I tell you that this man, rather than the other, went home justified before God. For everyone who exalts himself will be humbled, and he who humbles himself will be exalted."

In this parable we see two very different people. The Pharisee was a well-respected, self-righteous spiritual leader. The tax collector, on the other hand, was probably a liar, cheat and thief. The Pharisee had spent his life learning how to be good. The tax collector had used his position to receive financial gain. We could fully expect Jesus to tell a story about how the Pharisee would be blessed for his goodness. But Jesus didn't do that. Instead, the "punch line" of his story was that the tax collector received the blessing instead of the Pharisee. Why?

In his prayer the Pharisee drew attention to himself by telling God (and anyone listening) how good he was. He was, if you will, a braggart. From the story we notice two things about him. First, he seemingly lived a good life to inform the world that he was good in and of himself. And second, he talked about what he offered to God and humanity ("see what I give?") while needing nothing in return. He had it all.

The tax collector prayed in an opposite way from the Pharisee. Where the Pharisee stood tall before God, the tax collector could not even raise his eyes to heaven. Instead, he beat himself on the breast and begged God to have mercy on him. He drew God's loving and compassionate attention by telling God that he was a sinner in need of God's grace. He came with empty hands, in need of God's mercy.

This parable underscores two points about how we are to approach God. We begin by approaching God with an understanding of who he is. And then, we are to approach God with an understanding of who we are. We are sinners at the core—poor and frail in our abilities. We need God. We don't need to convince God how good we are, or that we can be independent from him. Good communication occurs when two individuals understand each other. God already knows us, for he created us and made himself available to us. If we want God to hear us, we must learn to approach God as sinner, not Pharisee.

Small group prayer will be enhanced when we begin and end with a clear understanding of our place before God. A group of truly humble people will be powerful in prayer. "Blessed are the poor in spirit."

MEETING EACH OTHER IN PRAYER

True prayer belongs in the small group because its effects are enhanced in community. Prayer allows a group to learn more about God. Small group prayer also helps people know each other better.

When we share communication with God, we are also communicating with each other. In prayer our greatest desires often pour forth. We exchange, with God and each other, our vision, love for God and motivation to follow him. Listening to a new believer pray is like receiving a breath of fresh air. Hearing a mature believer converse with the master becomes a rich experience. Sharing prayer with teachers, young mothers, teens, construction workers and other kinds of persons, helps you understand their world much better.

Small group prayer also gives structure to the rejoicing, suffering body of Christ spoken of in 1 Corinthians 12. It is difficult to get a fellowship or congregation of eighty—or 250 or 1,000—to identify intimately with your struggles and joys. In groups, however, we can learn to freely share together in prayer with close friends. People who share prayer needs and joys in a small group are loved and cared for.

WHAT IS PRAYER?

Prayer is our attempt to communicate with God through worship, confession and petition. And the purpose of prayer is, through intentional communication with God, to get to know God while worshiping him and asking him to act in response to our requests.

You will notice that we don't say that the purpose of prayer is to ask God to act on our behalf. Instead, the purpose of prayer is to get to know God while we worship and make our requests. The primary focus in prayer is our relationship with God.

In this definition, I have listed three things that we do in prayer—worship, confession and petition. Prayer can take any number of forms, and will vary with each unique God-human relationship, but these three broad categories cover what is communicated. Since we discussed worship in chapter nine, we will cover confession and petition in this chapter.

CONFESSION

The first response to worship is penitence. In Isaiah 6, the prophet Isaiah had a vision of the Lord. He saw God seated on a throne, surrounded by angels singing his praises. At the sight, he cried out in terror, "Woe to me! . . . I am ruined! For I am a man of unclean lips, and I live among a people of unclean lips, and my eyes have seen the King, the LORD Almighty" (v. 5).

Why does confession come from worship? Quite simply, a sinful person comes into contact with a loving and pure Being. We are laid bare. Fancy suits, high-powered executive positions, and vacation homes don't help at all. As the tax collector stood before God in humility, so we also must stand.

You may wonder why we need to confess if we have already asked Christ into our lives, and he has forgiven our sins. On an objective level, Christ's work on the cross, and his forgiveness of our sins, is complete. Psalm 103:12 proclaims that "as far as the east is from the west, so far has he removed our transgressions from us."

However, on a subjective level, we confess our sins to God not for redemptive (sins forgiven) means but for restorative (relationship made whole) means. When we sin, we damage our relationship with God. The apostle John says it this way: "If we claim to be without sin, we deceive ourselves and the truth is not in us. If we confess our sins, he is faithful and just and will forgive us our sins and purify us from all unrighteousness. If we claim we have not sinned, we make him out to be a liar and his word has no place in our lives" (1 John 1:8-10).

An example from a human-to-human relationship: Mike lies to Steve, and Steve finds out. Even though Mike may be fairly sure that he will be forgiven, there is no way that Steve can just shrug off the hurt. Mike has breached the special trust involved in friendship, and must request forgiveness if the relationship is to become strong again.

The same is true with sin. When we sin, we defy the law of God. Yet we want to be God's friend. From a relational aspect, we need to come with heartfelt repentance and a desire to be the kind of friend that we have been called to be.

We don't need to be unreasonable in confession, however. We could spend the better part of a day confessing individual sins, and focusing exclusively on sin can be counterproductive (leading to obsession). Our purpose in confession is to remind ourselves of God's grace offered through Jesus Christ, and to return (like the prodigal son) to that place of love and safety. We know the sins that hinder that relationship (whether pride, greed, lust, or any number of others), and we can confess these. Then, on a more general level, we can approach God as the tax collector: "God, be merciful to me, a sinner."

How can we offer safe times of confession in a group? Here are some ideas.

• Provide a safe place for confession. If your group has judgmental people, or an individual who breaches group confidences, you should not encourage confession until the problem or the individual has been dealt with.

• The application time of a study provides a great opportunity for confession. Simply ask the question, "How is God convicting or challenging you in relation to what we have studied?" Another great application question: "What do you believe God wants to do in your life in the next day, week or month?"

• A surprising aspect of group life is that many specific confessions will occur within the context of sharing or conversation. For example, in the midst of a group sharing time a woman may say, with a knowing glance at her husband, "Well, of course, some people here believe that I don't manage my time well . . . " Allow her to speak, and if no further clarification is offered by the couple, simply move on. At times, however, you may gently speak to her after the meeting and ask if she would like to talk about what she meant. That discussion might lead into confession or, in the case of a damaged marital relationship, healing.

• Groups may also employ silent times of confession as part of a prayer or worship time. Allow people to individually bring their sins to God in the quiet of their hearts, perhaps opening the time by reading a Scripture that offers the hope of the gospel of Christ (Eph 2:1-10).

• Finally, at key times in a group's life, perhaps before your group breaks for the summer, you might ask a more revealing question: "If you could receive one wish from God, something that he would change in your character or life, what would it be?"

PETITION

Along with confession and worship, we make requests of God in prayer. In practice most of our prayers take very little time before we start petitioning God. Many prayers go something like this: "Dear God, thank you that we can be here. Now, we pray that you would . . ."

We are expected to make requests of God. However, we are communicating with a Person, not a robot. You might place an order at a drive-in window without exchanging pleasantries, but you cannot carry on a fulfilling relationship without meaningful dialogue. For that reason we first address worship and confession before speaking of petition.

When you know God and feel close to him, you can have great confidence talking to him about what you need. In fact, the more you know and love God, the more your desires begin to fall in line with his will. You will end up praying for what God already wants. John 15:7 says, "If you remain in me and my words remain in you, ask whatever you wish, and it will be given you."

When making our petitions, we naturally focus our attention on three distinct areas—self, others and special needs.

Praying for ourselves. Many people feel uncomfortable when praying for themselves because they feel that their prayers are somehow selfish. Of course, this might be the case if you are naturally self-obsessive or you're praying for cars, homes, money, power and other such human toys. But in the areas of Christian growth and effectiveness, and provision and protection, you must request God's help so that you may thank God for how he responds.

Your first prayer for yourself should be in the area of Christian growth and effectiveness. Each day you have the opportunity to consecrate yourself to God and ask for help from the Holy Spirit. In Jesus' model prayer, the Lord's Prayer, he prays for God's kingdom to come and God's will to be done. God's kingdom will not become a reality until you learn to live in obedience to God the King. And God's will must first be done in your life before you can expect it to be done in the lives of others.

Then, you can also pray for God's provision and protection. The Lord's Prayer includes petition for daily bread and protection from temptation.

Groups should provide some opportunity for people to pray for themselves, or to request prayer. Perhaps on a special occasion, or during a group prayer time, you may invite members to simply pray to God about themselves: what God is doing, what they hope and long for, what causes them concern or anxiety, and so on. You may be surprised at the simple, childlike expressions of trust that are being offered.

Praying for others. We live in a world of need. We watch people suffer, observe tension in homes, and painfully observe the results of a world that in its lifestyle and choices has ignored God. Each person reading this chapter could conceivably spend ten hours per day praying for others and still have things to pray for. This need prompts our prayers for personal reconciliation; for family, friends or work associates to meet Jesus Christ; for our churches to experience renewal through the Holy Spirit; for the mission of the church to go forth into all parts of the world; and for healing. When we pray for others, we expand our personal prayers for Christian growth, provision and protection to others.

In prayer, love for others often finds its greatest expression, for we invest our time in secret for another's benefit. Apart from prayer, we can very easily manipulate circumstances or people to get our way. But when we pray for others, we relinquish some of our personal control when asking for God's will to be done. True love seeks the best for others. Loving petition on another's behalf allows us to move beyond our own realm of thought and into God's. And God knows what is best.

Here are some ways to incorporate prayer for others into your group time.

• Include times of sharing and prayer in which group members list individual or known needs. Some groups, attempting to develop community and trust, at times limit the items shared to those that personally impact members of the group. Thus, for example, I may be aware that my distant uncle is having toe surgery, but I would not share that. I would share my concerns over an upcoming exam, or ask prayer for my mother dying of cancer, since both directly impact me and drive passionate prayer from, and for, me.

• Try starting a time of prayer by inviting people to *pray* their requests (bypassing sharing, or incorporating it into the prayer time).

• Keep a notebook of requests so that you can see how God responds to your prayers.

• Remember at times to incorporate prayer for the "empty chair," nonbelievers, missionaries sponsored by your congregation, world "hot spots" and other concerns beyond the immediate scope of your group.

Praying for special needs. Nobody can get through life without experiencing some degree of pain and suffering. As we mature in life, we learn that, no matter how well things seem to be going, hard times could always be lurking around the corner. And Christians are not exempt from pain. We have the same chance as anyone else to get cancer, or to be in a car accident. Christians struggle with depression and chemical dependency. Christians also experience the loss of loved ones.

But we do have one blessing that others may not experience. We are part of a body, the body of Christ. In 1 Corinthians 12:26, Paul says that "if one part suffers, every part suffers with it; if one part is honored, every part rejoices with it." We are not alone, in good times and bad. We have others who can share in our lives, tempering the good times by reminding us to continue to rely on God, and smoothing out the bad times by demonstrating God's love. Small groups that support their members through times of pain demonstrate precisely what this passage is about—God's people helping each other during hard times.

We are to pray to God in special times of need. Our first prayer is often for healing, whether emotional or spiritual. We want God to put things right, and this is not unreasonable. Our "Daddy" has the ability to make everything work out in the end. Our faith can grow when he answers our prayers according to our requests.

But our faith can also grow when his answers don't work out the way we would like them to. First Peter was written for those who were experiencing great suffering and persecution. But the apostle Peter is not concerned with God "fixing" things for his Jewish Christian friends so that they could enjoy life again. Instead, Peter reminded the believers again and again that they had a special calling before God (1 Pet 2:4-5), complete with benefits and responsibilities. Suffering, rather than bringing an end to things, brought great opportunity to grow in Christ (1 Pet 1:3-9). And this should also be our prayer— that suffering would allow us, and others, to grow strong in Christ.

In Acts, Peter and John were arrested for healing a crippled beggar and for using the occasion as an opportunity to spread the gospel. The temple court was convened, and the religious leaders listened in fury to how the people were continuing to follow the teachings of Jesus, whom they had put to death. Not knowing exactly what to do, they threatened Peter and John with terrible persecution if they continued preaching the gospel.

Peter and John took the threats seriously, and Acts 4:23-31 describes how they found other believers meeting in a small group and gave them the report. No doubt the young Christians were scared for their lives, and their prayer serves as a model prayer for how we respond to life's circumstances.

> Sovereign Lord, you made the heaven and the earth and the sea, and everything in them. You spoke by the Holy Spirit through the mouth of your servant, our father David:
>
> > "Why do the nations rage
> >   and the peoples plot in vain?
> > The kings of the earth take their stand
> >   and the rulers gather together
> > against the Lord
> >   and against his Anointed One."

Notice that they immediately reached for the One who is always in control. In worshiping, they were no doubt reassured. Then they proceeded to make their requests:

> Indeed Herod and Pontius Pilate met together with the Gentiles and the people of Israel in this city to conspire against your holy servant Jesus, whom you anointed. They did what your power and will had decided beforehand should happen. Now, Lord, consider their threats and enable your servants to speak your word with great boldness. Stretch out your hand to heal and perform miraculous signs and wonders through the name of your holy servant Jesus.

They first identified themselves with Jesus, who had also suffered. But they affirmed that God had been in control when Jesus had suffered, just as God was in control in these circumstances. Their requests proceeded from a knowledge of God's power and sovereignty.

Then, instead of asking for protection, and rather than asking God to change the hearts of the leaders and guards in the temple court, they prayed for boldness and effectiveness in ministry. We would probably have prayed for the situation to change in our favor; they asked that they would be enabled to use it as an opportunity to spread God's love.

Finally, notice the result of their prayer. "After they prayed, the place where they were meeting was shaken. And they were all filled with the Holy Spirit and spoke the word of God boldly" (Acts 4:31). God heard and answered their prayer. Each person went forth in peace, knowing that God was with them.

Like them, the end result of our prayer should be peace, a deep satisfaction that God has heard and will answer. Philippians 4:6-7 makes the exciting connection between prayer and peace: "Do not be anxious about anything, but in everything, by prayer and petition, with thanksgiving, present your requests to God. And the peace of God, which transcends all understanding, will guard your hearts and your minds in Christ Jesus." If you are not experiencing such peace, then you might memorize these verses and practice *leaving* your requests at Jesus' feet.

We can learn many lessons from such prayers as the one in Acts that we just examined (and there are more in Acts). We can, and should, pray for God's intervention. But the *focus* of our individual and group prayers can be that God will use every circumstance in life as an opportunity to exercise our faith. As God's friends, and as his children, we can approach him with our petitions, in full confidence that he will work things for our good (Rom 8:28).

Prayer for special needs should be exercised judiciously. The basic rule of thumb for this type of prayer is that the group understands that either the group or a particular individual is deeply and painfully impacted by what is occurring. Here are some examples of events that might lead to special prayer: death, significant loss (health, job, marriage, child) and potential calamity (natural disaster, crime).

How do we respond to these and other significant crises? First, by interrupting the regular meeting schedule in some manner. For example, you might skip the study in a particular session to go to prayer. Second, by coming together as a group and discussing the situation. Besides prayer, is there a special response called for (for example, in a time of loss, perhaps the group might offer baby-sitting, or house cleaning)? Third, when appropriate, by gently laying hands on the person who is suffering, and bearing the burden of love together.

SUGGESTIONS FOR SMALL GROUP PRAYER

Envision yourself as a small group leader with people who don't know how to pray or are intimidated by prayer. You are not going to start out with deep, joy-filled times of prayer. You might find group prayer to prove extremely awkward at first, but with practice you will find prayer can be the part of the small group that people look forward to the most. Here are some suggestions related to what you can pray for and how you can initiate group prayer.

Developing a prayer covenant. When a group is first meeting, and you want to cultivate an atmosphere of safety and prayerfulness, you might consider discussing and laying this covenant before your group for acceptance:

Recognizing that prayer can be awkward for some, we covenant together that

PRAYING IN THE SMALL GROUP

The following are some ways you can experience prayer as a group:

- Read a penitential psalm (for example, Ps 6; 32; 38; 51; 102; 130 or 143) before or during prayer. Spend time in individual or corporate confession.

- Regularly make time for the group to share things for which they are thankful. Acknowledge answered prayer and give thanks to God. Make personal sharing about struggle and growth issues a part of group time. Encourage the group to pray for each other by name. Spend time asking God to apply lessons learned in group time.

- Pray for revival in church and community. Pray for non-Christian friends and relatives. Pray for those who are suffering.

Many people are uncomfortable with group prayer; some or all of the following ground rules could ease some of the tension:

- When praying, we will get into groups of four for greater personal comfort.

- No member is required to pray out loud. You should only pray out loud when you feel free to do so. If there is a long silence during prayer time, don't panic.

- During the first five minutes of our prayer time, we will focus our personal and group prayer on seeking oneness with God.

- Prayer, like any form of communication, is learned. We will be free to practice praying in our small group setting.

- We will pray with confidence, remembering Romans 8:26-27: "We do not know what we ought to pray for, but the Spirit himself intercedes for us with groans that words cannot express. And he who searches our hearts knows the mind of the Spirit, because the Spirit intercedes for the saints in accordance with God's will."

- the first three persons who pray during group prayer time will only use one sentence [encourages the "professional pray-ers" to be sensitive, and not to intimidate others]

- we will not hesitate to speak in brief sentences, or partial sentences [addresses the awkwardness that some people feel when praying in public]

- we will only pray when in groups of four [safety]

- we will make sure that we name in prayer each request made within our prayer time [so that people feel cared for]

Deciding what to pray for. To start with, you could occupy your time praying for each member of the group, asking God to help you grow in Christ. Groups grow stronger in bonds of love when they speak to God about each other *by name* in prayer. Then, you could pray for any of the following:

- Personal needs shared in the group
- Family and friends of group members
- The needs of your church or fellowship group
- Sick, shut-in, suffering or bereaved people that group members know
- Non-Christian friends, family and neighbors
- Missions and missionaries

You might also go back through the sections on worship, confession and petition and make your own list of possible prayer items.

Encouraging group prayer. As you think about how to encourage a spirit of prayer in the group, acknowledge the fears that many bring. While individuals do struggle praying to God, in groups the most significant fears about prayer are often based on what others think, rather than on what God thinks. As the group begins to feel more comfortable together, prayer will flow more naturally.

To start, you can open and close your meetings in prayer. When you open group meetings in prayer, you are consecrating the time to God and inviting his presence. When you close, you are offering yourselves to God and asking him to go with you. In the beginning, the burden for these prayers will often fall on the leader. You don't need to impress anybody with your prayers, least of all God. If you keep prayer simple and yet genuine, others will pray much more readily when given the opportunity.

If you want others to pray, make sure that you ask them before group time. Some people are embarrassed when asked in public. Rather than being a scary experience, group prayer should be an affirming exercise.

There are other ways to encourage prayer, especially in a group prayer time that comes as a scheduled part of the evening. For example, try holding hands when you pray as an expression of unity. Then you can pray around the circle, allowing some to squeeze the hands of the person next to them if they don't want to pray. Alternatively, allow free, conversational prayer so that those who want to can pray while others choose to pray silently. Or you can ask volunteers to pray for specific requests. And you can just start the prayer time and let the Holy Spirit lead. However you choose to pray, try to allow the group to develop its own unique ritual of prayer, one that stimulates freedom of expression in relationship with God.

PRACTICE MAKES PERFECT

Prayer in the small group will more readily become a reality if the leader is a praying person. If you worship God, keep the lines of communication open through confession and find freedom to bring your requests to God, then you will be the kind of person who encourages others to pray.

QUESTIONS FOR REVIEW

1. Do you know people you are unable to communicate with?

2. How do you feel when around them?

3. Why are "relationship" and "communication" such important concepts in prayer?

4. Why is it important to be humble when approaching God?

5. What is humility?

6. Why was the tax collector honored in Christ's story while the Pharisee was portrayed as wrong (pp. 182-84)?

7. What is your definition of prayer?

8. What do you think is prayer's purpose?

9. What happens when you confess sin?

10. When presenting petitions to God, how do you think faith in God's ability should be balanced with humble submission to God's will?

11. How did the Christians pray, in Acts 4, when faced with a threat to their lives?

12. How could this prayer guide your own?

13. How can prayer minister to the individual needs of people in a small group?

14. What are ways you can initiate praying in a small group?

READING FOR REFLECTION

Two great resources dealing with prayer are *Too Busy Not to Pray* by Bill Hybels (InterVarsity Press) and *Prayer: Finding the Heart's True Home* by Richard Foster (HarperSanFrancisco).

IDEAS FOR COACHES/TRAINERS

In small group ministry, one of the most exciting tools for building unity is sharing. Allow each person in your group to share his or her perception of prayer, as well as his or her struggles. The coach/leader can make sure that everyone in the group completes the following sentences (along with an explanation):

Part I: Individual Perception

- The first thing that comes to mind when I think of prayer is . . .
- One thing I wish that I felt more comfortable with in prayer is . . .
- When I think about my "prayer life," I feel . . .

Part II: Group Prayer

- Several things I have found helpful (or, think would be helpful) in encouraging group prayer are . . .
- Ways I think we could encourage shy nonprayers to participate in prayer are . . .

11

A MULTIPLYING COMMUNITY

A small group at First Church has met at Rachel's home for two years now. The group started with seven members, and all seven members still come. The weekly meetings are the highlight of the week for each individual. The Bible study is intense, the prayer victorious and the fellowship deep. God has used the group to bless each member, and they feel stronger in their faith as a result.

Rachel has proved to be an effective leader. She has faithfully kept the goal of discipleship before the group, encouraging them to take risks in their faith. She has allowed an honest, loving community to develop. And within the context of their caring community, the group has studied, worshiped, prayed and taken group outings together.

The group is studying Acts because they want to learn to identify with the early church. Like their early brothers and sisters in Christ, the small group meets in a home, eats together and enjoys talking about their Master. The study started with great promise, with group members reading a portion of Acts each day in their time alone with God.

Then Sam changed the direction of their study. The group had been inadvertently skipping over the practical emphasis of Acts — that the Holy Spirit was using the disciples to spread the gospel throughout the whole world (Acts 1:8). One Wednesday Sam came to the group with the following composition, which he felt that Acts 2:42-47 would say about the group:

> They focused their energy on the study of Scripture, because they were fascinated with what they were learning. Also, they couldn't wait to be together. Their meals and their prayer times were very enlightening. They got excited when they were together, exchanging hugs and talking about how they couldn't make it through a week without each other. Some of the members even allowed their study to bring positive change in various areas of their lives. For instance, when one member needed help, others would chip in, whether they needed money or sympathy or physical help. Each week they came together, but they also got together outside the group. Many called each other throughout the week, and they often had dinner together after church.
>
> Because of their love for each other and for God, the group felt close to God and enjoyed worshipping God. The pastor of the church was thrilled with the group because they were growing in their faith. But others in the church and world felt left out, for the group decided that it was better to stick with a proven group than to risk a new person ruining things for every one.

BLESSED TO BE A BLESSING

What was Sam pointing out in his version of Acts 2:42-47? He was chiding the group for being ingrown, enjoying God's blessings while withholding them from others.

Sam's honesty and willingness to ask tough questions led the group in a new direction with their study. The question that arose from his paraphrase was, *What would have happened if the early church had hoarded God's blessing, keeping it from others?*

The answer to the question is simple. The growth of the church would have been slowed or even stifled.

In the book of Acts, everything occurred within the context of God's ever-expanding kingdom. Acts 2 (echoed in other passages from Acts) contains a reference to people being saved: "And the Lord added to their number daily those who were being saved" (v. 47). Peter preached a sermon and people were saved. Believers met together in homes and others were saved. Christians met at the temple for prayer and the Lord added to the church. The church was scattered through persecution, and the worshiping, praying, studying community of faith went forth into the world to make other disciples.

Just as the early church was blessed so that they could carry God's blessing to others, small groups are a significant means through which people can be brought to Christ.

THE VISION FOR SMALL GROUP EVANGELISM

One of the most exciting stories circulating in the church today is how small groups (cells) are being used in many nations to fuel astounding growth. Massive cell group churches (that is, multiplying small group cells combined with weekly celebration) are located in Brazil, Indonesia, Korea, Kenya and many other nations. Using a few biblically based disciplines, including prayer, small groups and small group evangelism, some churches have achieved membership in the hundreds of thousands (compared to the largest congregations in America, which number in the tens of thousands).

How did they grow so quickly? They encouraged each small group to pray for non-Christian friends, and they taught leaders how to lead people to Christ. When each group leads people to Christ each year, geometric growth occurs.

What does this mean for your church or fellowship? A group of people, meeting together weekly, can start by praying for a non-Christian friend, knowing that they will want this friend to eventually join their small group and come into the faith and, ultimately, the church. Sooner or later the prayers will start to work, and the small group members will be moved by God to put love into action. The potential convert will be invited to the group and, surrounded by love, will respond with faith. In this way the small group can be used to touch one life for Christ.

How many small groups are part of your church or fellowship? Ten? One hundred? Can you envision one new person coming to faith because of each existing group, each year? What a great victory that would be! By God's grace and power, churches in the Western world would again participate in vital ministry.

WHAT IS EVANGELISM?

Evangelism is the conscious attempt, through word and deed, to share the good news of Jesus Christ with others, so that they can become disciples of Christ.

To expand on this definition, we will first consider how evangelism involves a conscious effort, through word and deed, *to share the message*. Second, evangelism is sharing the good news of Jesus Christ with another. Therefore, we want to take a look at the *process* involved in sharing the Christian faith. And third, the goal of evangelism is that people will become disciples of Jesus Christ. In the final section we will talk about how *small groups* can help, not only to evangelize, but also to lead people into the process of discipleship.

The message of evangelism, called the "good news" in the New Testament, is that salvation has come through Jesus Christ. In John 10:10 Jesus said, "The thief comes only to steal and kill and destroy; I have come that they may have life, and have it to the full."

The message that we carry contains both an objective and subjective side. We not only must know what is true, but we must also allow that truth to influence and penetrate our own lives before we can be positive witnesses.

OUR PERSONAL AND CORPORATE WITNESS

If you want to lead someone to Christ, you first have to know what you are talking about. Do you remember the rappelling instructor in chapter three who had never gone over the edge of a cliff? We noted the absurdity of his presuming that he could lead others when he had no idea of the challenges that lay ahead. This same illustration applies in witnessing. If Jesus Christ has not made a difference in your life, indeed if you are not striving to grow in Christ, then witnessing becomes a very difficult proposition. There are a number of motives that may lead you to witness (including guilt and obligation), but none is as compelling as a deep love for God. The best witness flows from his love to you, and from your life to those around you.

You cannot understand the words of the gospel until they have touched your life. Objectively, they are true and full of meaning. Subjectively, they have no place in your life until you have accepted their truths and watched them transform you through the working of the Holy Spirit.

There are two key indicators of the work of Christ in your life. First, *you have fallen in love with God* and begun to develop a life of intimacy with him. This will be demonstrated in both your thoughts and your actions.

Examine the example found in Luke 7:36-50, where Jesus was anointed by a sinful woman while he was eating at the home of a Pharisee. This woman entered a home in which she was not welcome and approached Jesus unannounced. She wept over Jesus in front of all the guests. Then she lovingly washed his feet with her hair, spreading perfume on them as she bathed them.

When Simon, a Pharisee, wondered why Jesus let a sinful woman do this, Jesus said, "Two men owed money to a certain moneylender. One owed him five hundred denarii, and the other fifty. Neither of them had the money to pay him back, so he canceled the debts of both. Now which of them will love him more?" (Lk 7:41-42).

Simon replied, "I suppose the one who had the bigger debt canceled" (v. 43).

The woman was willing to expose herself to ridicule because she had been changed by Jesus and wanted to express her love. While anyone could question her previous life, nobody could question her love for Christ. In a similar manner, we can also demonstrate this sincere love for Christ as a witness to the world.

Witnessing to the world about the grace we receive is very relevant to group members who are beginning to sink their roots deeper into God's love in a loving community that studies, prays and worships. Lively, Spirit-filled small groups put people in touch with their Creator, and therefore they allow their people to be more effective witnesses simply because they are growing in Christ. When people's lives are changed, they begin to speak to their work associates, friends and family about the impact their group and their Lord are having.

Your love for God will, sooner or later, cause you to view human relationships in a new light. So the second evidence of a changed life is that *you are growing in your ability to love others.*

Colossians 3:1-4 commands us to set our hearts and minds on things above. And what are those things? "Compassion, kindness, humility, gentleness and patience. . . . And over all these virtues put on love" (3:12, 14). As God works in our lives, change is produced in human relationships.

Compassion and love, among other traits, are important in witnessing. People respond to love much more readily than to ideas and concepts. You can try to witness to people by sticking tracts in their faces and demanding answers, or you can witness by developing loving relationships and demonstrating that Jesus is the reason you act as you do.

Small groups allow this personal means of communication to complement the objective truth of the gospel. Small groups encourage people to love God. They also teach people how to love one another. Without perhaps knowing it, they are preparing people to be effective witnesses of Jesus Christ!

THE GROWTH OF A GROUP'S LOVING, CARING WITNESS

- A foundation of love, caring, and good, open communication

- Significant experiences of God through study and worship

- Casual conversation about "my group" in positive, glowing terms

- A group commitment to praying for non-Christian friends

- Regular exploration of issues that directly relate to a witness at life and work, specifically by studying and praying about issues related to ethics, integrity, relationships and compassion

- Group study on being a winsome Christian witnesses

THE SPOKEN MESSAGE

So perhaps a non-Christian has entered your small group and is turned on by the genuine love that can be found in your midst. Now what?

Sooner or later you will need to verbalize the objective representation of the gospel so that others can receive Christ as their Savior as well.

Many devoted followers of Christ do not know how to lead another person into a saving relationship with God. If this is true of you or your group, make use of some of tools. These include Campus Crusade's "Four Spiritual Laws," The Navigators' Bridge model, and InterVarsity Christian Fellowship's outline "First Steps to God." These different methods present in a simple manner the process by which individuals can give their lives to Christ.

The key facts to remember are (1) we are sinners; (2) we need Christ to save us from our sin; (3) we must respond to Jesus by inviting him to be our Lord. Once we acknowledge Jesus Christ as Lord, we are to seek to live as children of God for the rest of our lives.

You can begin to see how small groups are perhaps the most effective way to bring evangelism into focus today. But the message is only part of the story of evangelism.

THE PROCESS

Very few people come to faith by picking up a Bible and reading it. Indeed, most people respond to Jesus Christ because they see the Christian life being lived out (subjective message); they have become aware of the truths necessary to become a Christian (objective message); and they have been loved by a Christian (the process).

In most cases, multiple persons are involved in the salvation of just one person. Perhaps a few friends and family members prayed. Maybe a vacation Bible school teacher took a continued interest in sharing the faith, as well as a high school teacher and college classmate. Then finally, a friend or spouse brought things together and prayed with that person for salvation. Jesus told his disciples in John 4:38 "I sent you to reap what you have not worked for. Others have done the hard work, and you have reaped the benefits of their labor."

For the sake of simplicity, let's pretend that there are only three relationships involved in the witnessing process, as in the following model:

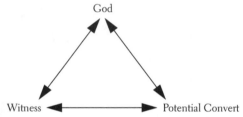

The arrows in the diagram show that each of the three individuals is related to the others. Each individual relates to the others through both give and take.

The place to start in the process is with God's part. God is the power behind the salvation of an individual. Jesus said in John 6:44, "No one can come to me unless the Father who sent me draws him, and I will raise him up at the last day."

When we pray for the salvation of a person, we pray believing that God is not only involved working through us, he is also involved directly in the life of the person we are praying for. God the Holy Spirit convicts people of their sin and need for God, and he slowly draws people to himself.

God also works in and through the life of a witness. He leads us to specific relationships, puts a burden for particular people upon our hearts and gives us the right words when we speak. God wants to use us to bring the salvation message to others.

Our response to God's role in the process of evangelism is simple—obedience. We know that he is powerful enough to change lives, and loving enough to know what people need. What he uses are vessels who can bring his life-changing Word to those in need. For a willing small group, evangelism always begins with prayer and proceeds as we obey the Lord's prompting.

The witness serves as a complement to God's part in evangelism. God uses witnesses who are willing to reach out in humility, love and confidence. Paul describes the evangelistic relationship that he had with the Thessalonians:

> For we know, brothers loved by God, that he has chosen you, because our gospel came to you not simply with words, but also with power, with the Holy Spirit and with deep conviction. You know how we lived among you for your sake. You became imitators of us and of the Lord. (1 Thess 1:4-6)

> As apostles of Christ we could have been a burden to you, but we were gentle among you, like a mother caring for her little children. We loved you so much that we were delighted to share with you not only the gospel of God but our lives as well, because you had become so dear to us. Surely you remember, brothers, our toil and hardship; we worked night and day in order not to be a burden to anyone while we preached the gospel of God to you. (1 Thess 2:6-9)

The witnesses in this passage were willing to give everything, including their very beings, to bring people to Christ. In John 15:13 Jesus says that the greatest love one can give another is to lay down one's life for another. But if our life is the greatest gift we can give, it is also the most difficult. The needs we naturally seek to meet are our own.

This creates a dilemma. In witnessing we want another person to experience the same joy we have found in Christ. But even though this appears to be selfless, there is the real possibility for selfishness and manipulation to enter the process. So we emphasize the following three biblical attitudes:

• *Humility.* The focus in evangelism should be the potential convert, not the witness. We often worry about how we look and whether we'll know what to say. Instead, we must seek the heart of God and learn to identify with others by putting them first, thus taking the spotlight off of us.

• *Love.* God will often call forth from the witness sacrifice and risk (elements of love). Responding to God's call can make us feel uncomfortable, out of our comfort zone. For example, we might risk rejection when sharing with a friend; or we might find that a person who has started to respond to the love of Christ turns on us out of fear. In these and other cases, to continue to witness to Christ's love doesn't mean that we get in people's faces and turn them away. It might mean, however, that the cost of the love we give has just gone up and we need to sensitively take one more step of sharing, or listening, or caring, than we normally might. When we do, and a person responds to God's love as a result, we see true love in action, the motive of our witness.

• *Confidence.* A witness can be confident in the power of God and the effectiveness of love. Even when mistakes are made on our part, we believe that God can work through barriers, and we look forward to the joy that will be his or hers when a person responds in faith. God will use our weakness as well as our strength.

Remember the parable of the sower in Matthew 13? Jesus told about a farmer who went out to plant seed in a field. Some seed fell on hard soil, some on rocky, some among weeds and some in good soil. Jesus ended the parable by saying, "He who has ears, let him hear" (13:9). The point of the story is that some people are ready to hear the gospel message; others are unprepared.

We are to plant seeds, which represent the objective and subjective message of the gospel and have been nurtured in humility and love. Then we can wait patiently for God to prepare the right hearts at the right time.

PLANTING SEEDS WITH GOD AND THE GROUP

- Choose the best group outreach format for your group. Open groups are free to invite new members at any time (subject to group agreement). Open/closed groups invite members at key junctures in group life, like when starting a new study or after a summer break; then they close to build unity and community.

- Target nonbelieving family, friends and work associates for prayer. Choose several names for targeted prayer, or invite each member to target one or two friends for prayer, and share the names with the group.

- Invite non-Christians into your group. Your group needs to be friendly and safe; minimize inside jokes among the Christian group members, and maximize communication and sharing. Choose a study that explores who Jesus is and what Jesus does (for example, the Gospel of Mark or a seeker study guide).

- Become a seeker small group. Nonbelievers should outnumber believers in such a setting. (For more information on this type of group—and indeed, the entire scope of small group outreach—see my book *Small Group Outreach*.)

- Participate as a group in a service or crosscultural experience (see chapter twelve).

MULTIPLICATION

At some point, a healthy group with an outreach mentality will grow too large. When that occurs, the group is perhaps ready to birth a new group.

We have noted on several occasions in this book that all cell and metachurch groups, as well as groups in many other configurations, include the recruitment of an apprentice leader in addition to a leader. They do this so that the group may birth a new group at some point in its future. Congregations and fellowships with multiplying groups typically develop leadership structures to support group leaders (many call that level "coach" or "mentor"), so that groups may receive coaching when working on group multiplication and leadership development.

There are several key items to keep in mind if your group is to multiply. You may learn more about group multiplication by reading *Small Group Outreach* or cell church and metachurch resources already listed in previous chapters, but here are some thoughts:

• Communicate the intention to birth from the first day a group meets. In the first covenant (see chapter four) that you provide new groups, clearly articulate that the purpose of this group is to multiply. Identify the leader and apprentice, and explain how multiplication will work.

• Develop a plan to train leaders and apprentice leaders. *The Big Book on Small Groups* is a training guide and could prove helpful whether the training occurs in a classroom setting, with a coach, or simply as one leader trains another.

• Identify potential birth timing. Some congregations require groups to birth within a particular time frame, or they disband them. Others let each group find its own way with staff/coaching guidance along the way.

• Encourage flexible birthing based on leadership realities within individual groups. You may choose to follow a mother-daughter birthing process (mother remains as larger group; daughter, with apprentice leader, forms a second small group). Or you may find, especially with very successful leaders, that a daughter-mother birthing is best (apprentice remains with larger group; leader leaves with small group). Sometimes an individual leader or apprentice leaves to form a new group. And every now and then, an entire group prepares each member to form a new group (turbo group).

• Identify transition/termination issues. Birthing new groups can be traumatic. Groups going through such transition need care, coaching and guidance. Help them to spend time listening and caring within the group. Encourage them to celebrate the past and embrace the future. Develop with them some termination activities, perhaps including a one-time celebration or a series of several gatherings.

PRINCIPLES OF SMALL GROUP EVANGELISM

As you begin to implement small group evangelism in your church, here are a few principles that can help:

Remember that the goal of small group ministry, and of evangelism, is to make disciples. When new people come into a group, they enter into a context of growth and challenge. Your job is not just to "win" people. It is also to nurture them into maturity. This is why small groups, with their emphasis on disciple-making, are ideal places for people to come to faith in Christ.

The leader can have a grand vision for evangelism, yet until the small group is ready they will not respond. Prayer prepares the group's heart and your own heart. You may discover that creating an outreach mentality may take months before the group is ready to respond. Keep sharing your vision for evangelism, but don't push your agenda onto the group.

CREATING AN EVANGELISTIC MINDSET

Here are some things that are helpful to think through when becoming an evangelizing small group:

1. Who are we targeting?

   a. Neighbors

   b. Nearby family

   c. Friends

   d. Work associates

   e. Church friends

   f. Community acquaintances

2. What can we do to stimulate evangelism within our group?

   a. Place an empty chair at each meeting as a constant reminder that our group must share its blessing. Pray for the person who is to sit in that chair.

   b. Pray for those listed above who don't know Christ. Agree as a group to pray for a certain person (or persons).

   c. Study what Scripture has to say about evangelism.

   d. Read a book on evangelism.

   e. Under God's direction, plan when to invite a person, what you are going to do during group time when he or she comes, and how you can effectively reach him or her with the gospel.

A healthy group is necessary for effective small group evangelism to occur. You don't want to bring people into a group that backbites, fights, or has other unhealthy elements. No group is perfect, but groups should be functional and healthy.

Evangelism needs to be intentional. Whether you are doing service projects or inviting several non-Christians into the group, have planning meetings in which you brainstorm answers to "who, what, where, when, how and why."

A growing, evangelistic small group ministry will soon begin to burst at the seams. When groups grow past twelve members, they tend to become less intimate and more confusing. The group leader should be prepared for this (it is a sign that you are doing a good job!) and nurture leaders who are prepared to lead the new groups.

INCORPORATING EVANGELISM IN SMALL GROUPS

Here are a few final thoughts about incorporating evangelism into small groups.

First, *start with prayer.* Pray that the group becomes an evangelizing group. Then, when group members' hearts are prepared to move forward in evangelism, the group can start praying for a few people to come to faith.

In order to emphasize that your group is one of the means that God uses to bring people to faith, consider praying for people that at least one group member has frequent contact with. This allows you to get updates and "coach" the person(s) in frequent contact with the potential convert.

Next, you could use what Lyman Coleman of Serendipity calls the *empty chair.* Put an empty chair into the circle at each meeting and either at the opening or closing prayer pray for the person who is to inhabit that chair.

The group could *do a study together* on either small group evangelism or evangelism in general. Along the same lines, you could memorize Scripture verses or work your way through an evangelism "technique." These will prepare you to give the objective message of the gospel.

You can also make choices about how exactly you plan to implement evangelism. Some groups will "disband" and recast themselves specifically as seeker Bible studies. These groups may choose to work through the Gospel of John or another Gospel by focusing on what can be learned about the person of Christ.

Other groups will maintain themselves as traditional cell groups open to inviting people into the group. These groups, while not always focusing on evangelistic themes, will choose topics relevant to all and will shower potential converts with love.

You and your group can have fun exploring these and other ways to share the good news of Jesus Christ with people who need to find true hope. May God bless you as, acting in humility, reaching out in love and demonstrating Christ in confidence, you share the message of Christ in its objective and subjective truth so that people respond in faith and become his disciples.

QUESTIONS FOR REVIEW

1. What do you think of the point Sam was making in the story at the beginning of this chapter?

2. Do you think his criticism applies to the church at large? Why or why not? To small group ministry? To your church or fellowship? To your small groups?

3. How would you define evangelism?

4. Is evangelism something that you feel confident doing? Why or why not?

5. What do we mean by "subjective message"? "objective message"?

6. Why do you think the subjective message of salvation is placed before the objective message in this chapter?

7. What is God's role in evangelism?

8. How can the one sharing his or her faith include God in the process of evangelism?

9. Who are people you are well acquainted with whom you can start praying for now?

10.What is the most important thing you learned from this chapter?

READING FOR REFLECTION

You can choose from many outreach and evangelism resources, including many already mentioned: *Small Group Outreach* by Jeff Arnold (InterVarsity Press); *Your Home, a Lighthouse* by Bob and Betty Jacks (NavPress); video courses/books/training materials such as Bill Hybels's *Becoming a Contagious Christian*; parachurch resources like the "Four Spiritual Laws."

IDEAS FOR COACHES/TRAINERS

Seeker Bible Study Role-Play

Leading a seeker Bible study is not necessarily a difficult task. In fact, you might be surprised at how fun and exciting it can be. For your role-play, first you will need a leader, preferably the one who feels most comfortable in the role of Bible study leader. Next, you will need someone to play a non-Christian. This person should be fairly imaginative, realistic and *not* overly dramatic. He or she will choose one of the roles listed below, tell the group what he or she has chosen, and then assume the part of a non-Christian who has been invited to the group. The rest of the group will play the part of group members (which shouldn't be too difficult, since you already are!).

For the next forty minutes, you will have a simulated Bible study. You will each turn to Mark 1 and discuss everything in the chapter that you can discover about Jesus. (Answer the question "Who is Jesus, and what does he do in the course of this chapter?") Pretend that you are investigators finding things for the first time (chances are that you will anyway!). Walk with Jesus for a time, see what he did, and try to understand why. You will hopefully observe that your non-Christian friend is actively engaged along with you.

After forty minutes are completed, discuss and evaluate this experience for your remaining five minutes. How did group members feel? How did the non-Christian feel? What could be done differently to make the Bible study even more engaging?

Roles for the Non-Christian

- You are the neighbor of one of the members and have come more out of curiosity than anything. You are divorced and have been feeling lonely.

- You are a self-proclaimed "agnostic," who reached that decision at great personal expense. You wish, deep down, that there was some form of Truth upon which you could cling. You were reared in a Unitarian home and have felt in the past that Christianity is too exclusive.

- You are an older adult with five grown children, and lately you have been feeling dissatisfied with your life. You are looking for answers and meaning. You are a person who made a very questionable commitment to Christ many years ago. You feel miserable, and now wonder why God would want such a weak person as you.

- You are a bright college student who has recently attended this church and been invited to the group. You are presently in a freshman philosophy course and your parents' moral values have been called into question. You are excited to have been invited to this meeting.

12

A MISSION-ORIENTED COMMUNITY

India's heavy rains had swollen the river until it was a torrent. As the Indian guides stood on the riverbank, they decided they would not risk crossing until the water receded. However, Granny Brand, the elderly missionary they were escorting to a meeting on the other side, pleaded with them to cross the river anyway. She was determined to make the meeting at all costs, for her services were needed. The guides smiled but shook their heads. They turned and started to walk away, only to be brought back by a cry. The old lady had tottered to the river edge on her walking sticks, plunged into the water and was on her way downstream. The guides rescued her and, impressed by her indomitable spirit, found a crossing point and brought her safely to the other side.

The story of Granny Brand, missionary to India in the 1900s, is a challenging chapter in world mission. She had gone to India and started a family with her husband, only to lose him to an illness. Instead of returning home to England in defeat, she had continued the mission, raised her children and ministered to the five mountain ranges that she and her husband felt God had called them to. She worked until she died, traversing the mountain ranges until in her nineties, sharing Christ's love with people who came to revere both her and her Lord. No river could turn her back.

Then there is the story of her predecessor in India, William Carey. Appropriately named the "Father of Modern Missions," Carey turned the eyes of an ingrown church to a world lost in darkness.

He was a cobbler in England in the 1700s. He loved God and had a deep concern for people in the world who did not know Christ. At that time, only the Roman Catholic Church did any major mission work.

Carey loved geography and fashioned a globe over which he could pray. This passion for prayer led Carey to India, where he preached, translated the Bible, taught agricultural techniques and put many of his other talents to good use. A fellow missionary gave this description of Carey near the end of his life:

> The brethren in Serampore are men to be wondered at: I speak of Carey, Marshman and Ward; or, if you will, Peter, James, and John. The former is most remarkable for his humility; he is a very superior man, and appears to know nothing about it. The great man and the little child unite in him, and, as far as I can see, he has attained to the happy art of ruling and overruling in connection with the others mentioned, without his asserting his authority, or others feeling their subjection; and all is done without the least appearance of design on his part. (E. Pritchett, Burman missionary, to a London friend, August 12, 1811)

What lofty descriptions are given this man. What beautiful determination we see in Granny Brand. They should be examples, not of heroes that we cannot be like, but of Christian people whom we can strive to imitate. For until every race, tribe and people group is evangelized, there is still work to be done. We need people of mission passion who can fuel such a work.

WHAT DO WE MEAN BY MISSION?

Mission is engaging in God's plan to redeem the world by extending his kingdom into every race, language and nation. This definition could, conceivably, also be used to describe evangelism. But for our purposes, the focus of evangelism is people you have everyday contact with. The emphasis in this chapter is on those with whom you would not ordinarily have contact. In other words, mission is cross-cultural.

Christians have debated for approximately the last hundred years about the relationship between the gospel message and social outreach. One group has tended to say that if people are starving, they need first to be fed before being evangelized, so the church's primary task in their view is to work for people's good. Another group has said that material need is never as important as spiritual need, so we must first take the gospel, and then worry about feeding people.

It doesn't matter who we are, or what we are doing—we must learn how to make disciples for Christ. A humble, loving, confident witness meets people's needs *while* living the gospel story. So the *goal* of mission is evangelism, but the *means* is compassion. Social concern and evangelism are not mutually exclusive. They are intricately linked together.

WHAT DOES MISSION HAVE TO DO WITH SMALL GROUPS?

Small group participants are usually members of a church who live in the same community or town. Mission involves reaching across cultures, doesn't it? So why would we even care about mission?

Here we start to unfold God's plan in its beauty:

> The LORD had said to Abram, "Leave your country, your peo-
> ple and your father's household and go to the land I will show
> you. I will make you into a great nation and I will bless you; I
> will make your name great, and you will be a blessing. I will
> bless those who bless you, and whoever curses you I will curse;
> and all peoples on earth will be blessed through you." (Gen
> 12:1-3)

God's plan for reaching the world was very simple. He promised
to bless Abraham (Abram's name after God changed it to mean "Father of many nations") so that Abraham could be a blessing to others.

This is what happens in the process of discipleship. If you are growing in Christ and receiving the benefits of God's blessing, sooner or
later God will give you a burden for those who are not saved (that is,
they have not yet received God's blessing). Several billion people on
earth have never received the claims of Christ. Many distinct groupings of people scattered throughout the world have not even heard the
gospel. They are called "unreached people groups."

Paul shares his passion for mission to unreached people in Romans
10:14-15:

> How, then, can they call on the one they have not believed
> in? And how can they believe in the one of whom they have
> not heard? And how can they hear without someone preach-
> ing to them? And how can they preach unless they are sent?
> As it is written, "How beautiful are the feet of those who bring
> good news!"

Just as with Paul, discipleship causes Christians to identify with
God's plan for the world. And that leads to action.

In Ephesians 3:10-11 Paul describes God's design for the church. "His intent was that now, through the church, the manifold wisdom of God should be made known to the rulers and authorities in the heavenly realms, according to his eternal purpose which he accomplished in Christ Jesus our Lord."

According to Ephesians 3:10, God's plan for the world is to be made known *through the church*. And what is that plan? "This mystery is that through the gospel the Gentiles are heirs together with Israel, *members together of one body, and sharers together in the promise in Christ Jesus*" (Eph 3:6, emphasis mine). In other words, the gospel will break through all barriers and bring together one worshiping, praying, loving body—the church.

And the result is this:

Consequently, you are no longer foreigners and aliens, but fellow citizens with God's people and members of God's household, built on the foundation of the apostles and prophets, with Christ Jesus himself as the chief cornerstone. In him the whole building is joined together and rises to become a holy temple in the Lord. And in him *you too are being built together to become a dwelling in which God lives by his Spirit.* (Eph 2:19-22, emphasis mine)

God's design is that the body of Christ will become a heavenly temple, inhabited by God and filled with tremendous joy.

When sin destroyed our fellowship with God, God sought to restore that communion by constructing a spiritual kingdom that would reclaim relationships one person at a time. And that is what the church must be doing. We are to go into every part of the world, reclaiming the earthly kingdom one person at a time by making disciples in community. As the church grows, we are filled with the very presence of God, becoming the "growing temple" that Paul spoke of.

And in this, we have come full circle. For you see, God's plan is for evangelism and mission to be *the result* of his blessing that comes through study, worship, prayer and community. He has brought salvation so that we would offer salvation to those who are lost. He has given us grace so that we would be burdened for those who do not experience his grace.

MISSION AND SMALL GROUPS

So you see why mission is so important. But what are you—a small group leader or member—to do with this knowledge? Should you uproot and move to the mission field? For many people, the answer is no. God will call people overseas whom he has specially prepared. For now, you are to be a faithful disciple where you are.

But then should we ignore study, worship and prayer to focus on mission and evangelism? The answer again is no. We need to be growing in our faith to be used by God. Of course, some groups will form specifically for the purpose of praying for mission, or doing mission. Most groups, however, will experience mission as part of group life.

Here are a few ideas that you can use as you see fit.

Learn. Through libraries and bookstores you may access wonderful mission books and biographies that the group can study. Also, the group could invite missionaries to speak to the group on occasion, and they could maintain correspondence with certain missionaries. The group might do a study on mission, learning about God's activity in the world through the Scripture. In addition, they could participate in a mission conference (among others, the Urbana Mission Convention is wonderful).

Pray. Perhaps the most significant thing that your group can do is pray. A faithful small group can do great things by releasing God's power in the world. The group could participate in or sponsor a "concert of prayer" (see David Bryant's *Concerts of Prayer* for ideas), or they could adopt a country, family or people group as their own group prayer concern. Then again, they could pray through a mission resource book like *Operation World*, learning about needs in different countries and continents. Like William Carey we can receive a vision for mission by using a globe and praying on behalf of the countries.

Support others. The group can get more intimately involved in mission by supporting others who are missionaries. They can adopt a missionary and offer prayer support. They could also raise funds to support short-term mission projects through your congregation, like those in which young people participate. Or they could organize a church mission conference to raise awareness of the missionaries who are supported by your church.

Go into the community. The most personal step that a group can take is to go. Remember that mission involves crossing cultures. Sometimes you can do that by merely walking across the street. Local mission could benefit from carpenters, lawyers, parents who can teach parenting skills, and financial experts who can teach budgeting. Do you have something that could benefit a local mission? It is worth the effort to find out.

Many of today's small groups have become familiar with the term "service evangelism." Service evangelism, popularized by Steve Sjogren's *Conspiracy of Kindness*, involves Christians giving "a cup of cold water in Jesus' name." Typical service projects include giving free car washes, passing out free soda at Little League baseball/softball games and raking leaves for shut-ins. The projects tend to be one-day, fun, highly relational, low risk and simple. They rely on willing hands and hearts.

The evangelism component of such projects is handled in two ways:

First, by presenting a small flyer that includes your fellowship name and address and a simple phrase like, "You have received this gift free, no strings attached, as an example of the love of Jesus; from your friends at First Church." Second, by the spontaneous conversations that invariably build due to the curiosity that people will have when they witness your group in action.

Your small group could also become a mission team, like those utilized by the well-known Church of the Savior in Washington, D.C. People who join the church are placed into teams that do everything from providing low-income housing to running a thrift shop. Using mission teams, they have ministries throughout Washington, and their ministry impact has been felt by many. By choosing to carry out a particular ministry, your small group can help fulfill the Great Commission right in your own community.

Go overseas short-term. Your church could send people on a short-term project, whether it be a church-planting project or a building project. Some or all of a small group could go. Think how much your small group would benefit if the whole group went away for a few weeks to serve God together!

Go overseas long-term. A member or two of your small group might end up being called to the mission field. You could help them affirm their call, as well as assist with fundraising, research and the many logistics that must be dealt with before someone can enter the mission field. Then, when they go forth from your group, you could lend continued prayer and financial support.

I WILL BLESS YOU AGAIN

God's promise to Abraham could have easily been amended to say, "Abraham, I will shower my blessing upon you as you study, pray and worship, in order that you can go forth as evangelists and mis-

CHOOSING A MISSION PROJECT

- What are burdens that members of our group possess for local or foreign mission?

- What needs exist that our group can address?

  Foreign mission—pray, support a missionary, go on a short-term mission trip, sponsor a mission emphasis week at church, or sponsor a child through Compassion or World Vision.

  Local mission—homelessness, poverty, drug and alcohol abuse, teen outreach, marriage counseling, hospice care, AIDS, abortion and adoption, and assisting internationals.

- What one or two ideas can our group agree upon?

- What financial obligations (think about mission support, supplies, food and so on) will we incur with our mission ideas? Have we checked with the church financial treasurer and pastor to make sure that we are acting in accordance with church financial guidelines?

sionaries in the world. Then, I will bless you even more deeply, for you are participating in the spread of my joy. I will add joy upon joy, blessing upon blessing, grace upon grace. You above all people will be blessed."

I can paraphrase this passage with confidence, because recognition of God's plan and purpose leads to fulfillment of that design, and this leads to joy. It feels good to know that you are pleasing God!

Don't ever lose sight of what you are doing and why you are doing it. Small group ministry is a way of extending God's kingdom into the world. When your group starts evangelizing and becoming interested in mission, you are ready to see second and third generations of disciples being made. May God bless you as you attempt to respond in obedience to this task.

QUESTIONS FOR REVIEW

1. Who are missionaries that you have heard of, and admired, for their obedience and passion?

2. How do you feel about mission? your involvement in mission?

3. How would you define mission?

4. How would you reconcile evangelism and social concern in mission if you were a crosscultural missionary?

5. What is God's plan for the church (Eph 3:10-11; 2:19-22)?

6. How, in this chapter on mission, have we come "full circle" from the beginning of the course?

7. What are ways that you can get others in a small group interested in mission?

8. Why do we receive joy when we fulfill God's plan for mission?

READING FOR REFLECTION

For further reading, see Steve Sjogren's *Conspiracy of Kindness* (Vine Books). See also Patrick Johnstone's *Operation World* (Zondervan); and when visiting a Christian bookstore, check out the mission and mission biography sections.

IDEAS FOR COACHES/TRAINERS

- Discuss different ways that your congregation would allow or encourage groups to participate in forms of mission.

- Brainstorm ten possible service evangelism projects. Choose one, and develop a plan that answers the questions who, what, why, when, where, how, how much.

- Try this role-play. Your group has been "elected" as the mission awareness committee for your church. This means that you are responsible for engaging as much of the church as possible in mission. You will want to select a mission chairperson to help you fulfill your responsibilities. He or she should be the one among you who is most outspoken about mission.

  You have two duties to perform in this next forty minutes:

  1. Brainstorm and come up with a list of local and foreign mission opportunities for church members. It is helpful to base your list on actual needs you are aware of (for instance, your community might have a number of homeless people, or a university where an international student ministry could be developed). Have a group "secretary" list the ideas under the headings "Local Mission Opportunities" and "Foreign Mission Opportunities." This list will be shared with the other groups who are doing the same role-play.

  2. Write a thirty- to sixty-second "spot" announcement as though someone from your committee would read it on a Sunday morning to get people excited about mission. You will want to refer in the spot to the fact that you have a compiled list of ideas. In addition, you may want to share what mission is, why it is important and what is expected of every church member in regard to mission. You may be called upon to share this announcement in the large group.

APPENDIX A
SMALL GROUP STARTER KIT

Every small group has to begin somewhere. This guide[1] has been created to help meet some early group needs. Thus, the guide enables the group to

- begin its initial steps toward becoming a biblically functioning community

- explore the idea of a small group, including its purpose and functions

- use Bible study in an interactive, relationship-building atmosphere

- use a mapped-out resource during its first four meetings so that the leader and members may relax and concentrate on building relationships

- apply healthy, relevant small group ideas and principles to enable a group to become strong from the very beginning

LEADING A GROUP THROUGH THE STARTER KIT

Little League baseball has its coaches. Classrooms have their teachers. Small groups must have leaders. You are an indispensable part of the disciple-making process.

---

[1]The purpose of the Small Group Starter Kit is to guide a small group through its first few meetings. In order for this resource to be of maximum use, every member should have a copy. Permission is given by the author (Jeff Arnold) and publisher (IVP) to photocopy appendix A for use in small groups only and not for resale © 1995 by Jeffrey Arnold.

Many groups have no leaders, and some of them do quite well. But in order for a leaderless group to work, too many things need to be close to perfection: the overall communication, the ability of the group to listen to its quieter members, the facilitation of the Bible study choices and the ability to deal with difficult group problems, among other things. Leaders help in these key areas, and more. Here are a few basic things you can consider to enhance your leadership.

Prayer. One of the most enduring pictures we have of Jesus Christ is that he was a man of prayer, continually on his knees before God. If you believe that only God can change a heart, help a group get past its difficult times and be present with each disciple throughout the week, then you should commit to praying daily for each group member. More than anything else you do, leading in prayer will have a great impact. If you need help in this area, there are many great books on the topic, such as *Daring to Draw Near* by John White (InterVarsity Press).

Logistics. Christians who are familiar with the working of the Spirit will understand that the Holy Spirit can work in the most difficult of conditions. That doesn't mean, however, that we should test God. For example, most groups would study better in a well-lit room without phones ringing and dogs jumping on people.

The small group leader can help to make sure that the place, time, room condition, refreshments and other sundry arrangements have been made and that the group will be comfortable as it learns and grows.

Stages. Every relationship goes through stages, so it stands to reason that groups will go through them as well. Experts generally recognize four stages where groups are concerned: honeymoon, conflict, community and closure. It helps if leaders are able to recognize the stages so that they do not try to downplay significant things that are happening (for instance, when conflict occurs and the leader wants to pretend that nothing is wrong). You can read more about growing through the stages in chapter seven.

Empowering members. A small group is not a lecture series. So if you find yourself talking too much, then you are probably holding your group back. There are several things you can do to ensure that you are leading properly.

- Delegate. The design of this four-week beginning is that you will delegate group roles in the first week of your group's life. You must make sure that people follow through on their duties, but don't do their work for them. Delegating will keep people coming (because they're needed), get people to exercise their gifts and bind your group together.

- Facilitate. The leader acts as a channel to make good things happen. When you facilitate a discussion, you help the group to learn for itself. When you facilitate in decision-making, you make people think for themselves. Facilitating is not easy, but can be made easier when you learn to ask probing questions (who, what, when, where, how, why).

- Be open. Because you want the group to learn and grow, you have the opportunity to learn and grow along with them. The group will go only as deep as the leader does. Do not remove yourself from the process of disciple-making. Instead, humbly and excitedly learn the lessons of the Christian faith with the rest of the group.

PREPARING TO LEAD A MEETING

1. Spend time in prayer. Ask God to help you understand and answer the questions. Pray for each member of the small group by name. Ask God to prosper your small group.

2. Carefully prepare for each study by reading and rereading the assigned Bible passage. If you are doing a book study, you may want to read through the entire book prior to the first study. This will give you a helpful overview of its contents.

3. This study guide is based on the New International Version of the Bible. It will help you and the group if you use this translation as the basis for your study and discussion. Encourage others to use the NIV as well, but allow them the freedom to use whatever translation they prefer.

4. Work through the questions in the study yourself. Formulate your responses so that you can lead the group to find its answers. Write your answers in the space provided, along with any notes that you wish to make. These can give you a quick reference during the study.

5. It might help to have a Bible dictionary handy, such as the *New Bible Dictionary*. Use it to look up any unfamiliar words, names or places. (For additional help on how to study a passage, see *Discovering the Bible for Yourself* [InterVarsity Press].)

LEADING THE MEETING

1. Begin the study on time. Unless you are leading an evangelistic Bible study, open with prayer, asking God to help you to understand and apply the passage.

2. Be sure that everyone in your group has a study guide. Encourage them to prepare beforehand for each discussion by working through the questions in the guide.

3. At the beginning of your first time together, explain that these studies are meant to be discussions, not lectures. Encourage the members of the group to participate. However, do not put pressure on

those who may be hesitant to speak during the first few sessions.

4. Read the introductory paragraph at the beginning of the discussion. This will orient the group to the passage being studied.

5. Read the passage aloud if you are studying one chapter or less. You may choose to do this yourself, or someone else may read if he or she has been asked to do so prior to the study. Longer passages may occasionally be read in parts at different times during the study. Some studies may cover several chapters. In such cases, reading aloud would probably take too much time, so the group members should simply read the assigned passages prior to the study.

6. As you begin to ask the questions in the guide, keep several things in mind. First, the questions are designed to be used just as they are written. If you wish, you may simply read them aloud to the group. Or you may prefer to express them in your own words. However, unnecessary rewording of the questions is not recommended.

   Second, the questions are intended to guide the group toward understanding and applying the main idea of the passage. There may be times when it is appropriate to deviate from the study guide—for example, a question may have already been answered. If so, move on to the next question. Or someone may raise an important question not covered in the guide. Take time to discuss it! The important thing is to use discretion. There may be many routes you can travel to reach the goal of the study. But the easiest route is usually the one the author has suggested.

7. Avoid answering your own questions. If necessary, repeat or rephrase them until they are clearly understood. An eager group quickly becomes passive and silent if they think the leader will do most of the talking.

8. Don't be afraid of silence. People may need time to think about

the question before formulating their answers.

9. Don't be content with just one answer. Ask, "What do the rest of you think?" or "Anything else?" until several people have given answers to the question.

10. Acknowledge all contributions. Try to be affirming whenever possible. Never reject an answer. If it is clearly wrong, ask, "Which verse led you to that conclusion?" or again, "What do the rest of you think?"

11. Don't expect every answer to be addressed to you, even though this will probably happen at first. As group members become more at ease, they will begin to truly interact with each other. This is one sign of a healthy discussion.

12. Don't be afraid of controversy. It can be very stimulating. If you don't resolve an issue completely, don't be frustrated. Move on and keep it in mind for later. A subsequent study may solve the problem.

13. Stick to the passage under consideration. It should be the source for answering the questions. Discourage the group from unnecessary cross-referencing. Likewise, stick to the subject and avoid going off on tangents.

14. Periodically summarize what the group has said about the passage. This helps to draw together the various ideas mentioned and gives continuity to the study. But don't preach.

15. Conclude your time together with conversational prayer. Be sure to ask God's help to apply those things which you learned in the study.

16. End on time.

Many more suggestions and helps are found in *How to Lead a*

LifeGuide® *Bible Study* (InterVarsity Press). Reading and studying that would be well worth your time.

SESSION 1
WHY SMALL GROUPS?

Imagine a man named Bob walking into your church or fellowship group. Bob is married, has two young children, is an engineer, lives in a modest housing development, has been active in church and is prepared to get involved in your church.

Bob is a Christian man not unlike others, facing a host of potential issues and problems in his life and faith: time management, marriage and extended family, parenting, relating to superiors at work, being a boss, living ethically in an immoral world, having a godly thought life, dealing with sin, and other issues.

These issues don't necessarily impact his effectiveness in the church. He could be involved in committees, for example, while his wife remains at home with the kids and his marriage falls apart. Perhaps nobody would ever know of sin areas or work struggles, because at many levels of the church, these issues don't enter conversation.

Your church is full of unique individuals like Bob, all with a complex set of "givens"—life situations, relationships, sin and addiction areas—that impact their lives and either hold back or stimulate their faith. How can a church best minister to all of its people when all of their needs are so varied and unique?

One exciting answer is small groups. In this first study we will explore the purpose of small groups and realize that small groups are for people like Bob who want to learn more about God and grow in their faith.

Community builder: Fun. The purpose of this activity is to help you get to know one another in a fun, nonthreatening manner. The object of this game is to (a) write things about yourself that you do not believe others in the group will know or can figure out, and (b) try to guess what others have written about themselves. The person who guesses the most about the others "wins."

Hand each person a piece of paper and pencil. On the paper each person is invited to write three things. First, a statement that is true about himself or herself (remember, try to think of things that others won't know). Second, a statement that is partially true (for example, if you've hiked in the mountains, you might "stretch" that a little bit and claim that you've hiked Mount Everest!). Third, an outright lie (*I am a rodeo rider*). Do not put your names on the papers.

The papers are folded and handed to the small group leader, who reads each one slowly, in turn. Group members hear the clues and try to guess, writing down the name of the person they think fits each set of clues until all papers have been read.

Then, the leader goes back through the pile, rereads them, and the group discusses who that person might be. Eventually, the real person "owns up." Group members either mark their guess right or wrong. The person who guessed the most right wins.

Discussion. Everyone should answer questions 2-4.

1. One of the most significant benefits that small groups provide is the opportunity to get to know people, as we just did. What kinds of groups have you been in before? (Consider church, work, sports, clubs and so forth.)

2. When you think about being in a small group, which most closely characterizes your feelings and why?

   ☐ I've been in lots of groups and am relaxed.

   ☐ This is my first small group experience, and I'm a little unsure.

   ☐ _____ [supply name] twisted my arm and I came.

☐ I'm apprehensive but excited.

☐ Other:

3. What are one or two things that you would like to see happen as a result of participating in this group?

Read Acts 2:42-47 together. List some (at least eight or nine) of the things that the early believers did as they grew together in their faith.

4. Of the items mentioned, which match your hoped-for results shared under question three above?

5. What kinds of things happened as a result of the new church's faith (vv. 43, 45, 47)?

6. What do you think it would have been like to participate in the Acts 2 church?

7. Disciples of Christ are growing to love God with heart, soul, mind and strength, and to love neighbors as they love themselves. On the "discipleship scale" I am [every member should tell where he or she is and why]

| barely alive | moving forward | learning the lessons | a disciple |

8. Like Bob in our first example, I have issues I would like help with. They are _____

_____

_____

Closing time of prayer. Allow each member to share one or two things that he or she would like to receive prayer for. Then allow the group to pray in sentence prayers.

Meeting Time and Place: _____

Meeting Frequency: _____

Ground Rules:

Everyone is important to this group. We will make sure that if someone is absent, we check in; if a person is to miss, that person is expected to call a group member before the meeting.

We welcome newcomers. We will place an empty chair at meetings, and discuss when and if new members may join.

We encourage sharing. Therefore, if our group has more than seven members at a meeting we will break into groups of four for sharing and prayer times.

We are accountable. Therefore we promise to be honest and affirming, we will use group consensus to make decisions, and we will not talk about each other unless the person being spoken of is present.

We understand that this group will eventually grow and multiply (become two groups).

Group Roles:

Leader: _____

Apprentice leader: _____

Host: _____

Prayer coordinator: _____

Other: _____

We agree to abide by the covenant these next few weeks as we seek to become a positive community of Jesus Christ.

Signed: _____

Sample Covenant

Housekeeping. Have the group read, discuss and approve the covenant (p. 239) to guide your next four weeks.

SESSION 2
A RELATIONSHIP-BUILDING COMMUNITY

Mark 10:35-45

Riding to work one day, I overheard the words of a rock song that went something like this: "Why can't we just love each other? Why can't we get along better? Just love each other, that's all we have to do."

Sounds pretty good to me. But the person who wrote those words must not be married.

If anyone thinks that love is, or should be, easy, then he or she should live under the same roof with the same person for a lifetime. Studies show the majority of new marriages will fall apart. Of the remaining ones, few will reach a stage of community that lasts.

The fact is that love is the most difficult thing that a person is called upon to do. Anything is easier: getting a master's degree, writing a theological treatise, designing a new computer, climbing Mount Everest.

Even the disciples found love difficult. After three years of living with God himself, watching the truest, most pure form of love demonstrated in history, they still didn't get it. Just one and a half months before the Day of Pentecost (when they were to assume their leadership role over the church), the disciples bickered over who was the greatest in the kingdom, and fought because nobody wanted to wash the others' feet (see the Gospel accounts of the Last Supper).

They knew how to jostle and position themselves, to soak Jesus' energy with their constant demands. They did not yet know how to serve, to reach beyond themselves and love another until they reached a stage of community that we will call *We like you because . . . We love you in spite of . . .*

Discussion

1. Who has been your longest and best friend?

2. Why has the friendship worked?

3. How many close friends do you have in your church or fellowship? Explain.

4. In the last session, we saw that the purpose of this small group is to make disciples. Before we can grow as disciples, we must be a healthy, loving community. In the New Testament the Greek word for community is *koinonia*. The apostle Paul used the word *koinonia* thirteen times. Each time he spoke of a Christian relationship that imitates Christ by producing the kind of love that acts for the good of the other. It creates bonds that cannot be destroyed. What kinds of things would a koinonia community do?

5. Contrast a koinonia community with a self-centered community by reading Mark 10:35-45. What did James and John request of Jesus (v. 37)? What do you think prompted their request?

6. How did the other disciples react (v. 41)? Why?

7. Jesus called the disciples together and taught a lesson on discipleship while addressing the motives behind the requests. In verse 43 what determines Christian greatness?

8. How does one become *first* (v. 44)?

9. How does service determine effectiveness in Christian relationships?

10. Through this experience and others, Jesus was able to teach the disciples that power and control are at the root of our struggles with one another. Surprisingly, the events of Mark 10 occurred after the disciples had been with Christ for a long time. Even more surprising, the disciples fought the same battle the very night of

the Last Supper (see John 13:1-17). What are ways that power and control struggles enter into our relationships?

11. Small group experts talk about stages that a small group will need to go through in order to become a true community. In each stage, power and control issues are present. For each of the stages that follow, list several ways that a Christlike servant might think and act.

- *Stage 1: Isn't this great?* The honeymoon stage encompasses unity at the expense of diversity. The group, like yours, is young. Everything is new; individual differences are minimized as the group begins working together. This is the *honeymoon stage.* In Mark 1:35-39 the disciples find Jesus in prayer and tell him that everyone is looking for him. They are pleased that Jesus is so successful!

- *Stage 2: Hey, you left your dirty laundry in the bathroom!* The conflict stage emphasizes diversity at the expense of unity. As time goes by, individuals begin to see areas where they are different from one another. People are tempted to gossip with each other outside of the group, and tension is felt. Subtle, and not so subtle, power struggles, as we saw in Mark 10:35-45, occur.

- *Stage 3: We like you because . . . and we love you in spite of . . .* In stage three there is community or unity alongside diversity. Groups that are honest with one another and are willing to pay whatever price is necessary reach this stage. Many groups settle into stage two with bickering and backbiting and never make it to this stage of unconditional love. In John 21:15-19 we see Jesus offer Peter his forgiveness after Peter denied Jesus. This is the action phase of a small group.

- *Stage 4: We're a team!* The closure stage affirms unity and brings the group to an end. Groups are not static entities. They are dynamic organisms that are born and will eventually either multiply or die. In Acts 2:1-4 the Holy Spirit comes to the disciples. The power of the Spirit enables them to disband and go out into the world in confidence. This was the culmination of ten days of intimate prayer, sharing and community building by the disciples. The ultimate goal of a group is to multiply in order to serve others.

12. What kinds of things can you do to help your group through the four stages?

13. One way to protect your group from power and control issues is by writing a good group covenant. You may remember that in study one you promised to be honest and affirming, to use group consensus when decisions are made and not to talk about one another apart from the group. This is the beginning of a covenant.

14. A second way to protect your group from power and control issues is by praying together. As you close in prayer, consider some of the ways that group members identified potential control issues that we face in relationships (question 10). Spend some time asking God to protect your group and to lead you into loving, healthy community so that you can be effective disciples of Jesus Christ.

SESSION 3
A GROWING COMMUNITY

Psalm 1

The headlines trumpet the news:

The stock of XYZ corporation plummeted 14 percent yesterday

on news of flat revenue and lower-than-expected earnings growth. XYZ corporation has been hurt by competition in their industry. Susan Smith, stock analyst with Take Stock America, downgraded XYZ to a sell. Meanwhile, XYZ's CEO, Bob Hutchins, promised that cost-cutting measures, company streamlining and increased productivity will turn his company around.

An interesting thing about investing in the stock market is that people will only invest in stocks that provide a return. Companies that don't grow are dropped like hot potatoes. In fact, the ultimate long-term fuel behind the rise in a stock's price is a rise in its sales and earnings. In the long term, growth is what the stock market is about.

Growth is what the Bible is about as well. If the status quo were to be maintained, then God would not have had to intervene in human history as often and as persistently as he has. Yet there are some small groups that study the Bible for years and never seem to produce spiritual or numerical growth. One of the charges leveled against small-group Bible studies is that tangents and academic intrigue are too often the fruit of study.

So there is a dilemma facing groups interested in making disciples: how to use the textbook of the Christian life in such a way that growth in knowledge ultimately leads to wisdom, grace and love. As Jesus said in Matthew 7:16, "By their fruit you will recognize them." This study is about finding that fruit.

Discussion

1. What was your favorite subject in school (any level) and why?
2. What is something you would like to do, study or know before leaving this life?

3. Read Psalm 1. In one or two sentences, what does this psalm seem to be saying?

4. There are three things that the "blessed man" does not do that are found in verse 1. List them in your own words.

5. Why do you think that people walk in the counsel of the wicked, stand in the way of sinners and sit in the seat of mockers?

6. Describe the result of the negative behavior exhibited in verse 1 (vv. 4, 6).

7. In verse 2, the blessed man does something that is good. What does it mean to *delight* in Scripture and to *meditate on it day and night*?

8. There are three blessings that come to the man who roots his life in Scripture (v. 3). In your own words, what are they?

9. In what forms may these blessings come in a person's life? Use examples if you can.

10. Based on what this psalm teaches, what would you say to a small group that studies the Bible endlessly, but whose members never seem to grow in their relationships with God and one another? to individuals who continually find themselves being led into sin by friends?

11. In order to grow in discipleship, this group needs to bathe itself in Scripture and to begin applying Scripture to all of life. What is an area of your life that God has changed?

12. What one area of your life would you like to see God begin to change in the coming year?

13. Write down the needs and concerns that were expressed in question 12 so that you can pray for one another. As you spend time

praying together, reflect on what the psalm means when it says to delight in God and his Word. As you pray for each other, you may want to open your Bibles to Psalm 1 and use words from it to frame your request. For example, "Lord, help us to delight ourselves in your Word."

SESSION 4

AN OUTREACHING COMMUNITY

John 4:4-38

When I walk into the home of a hunter, I see trophies on the wall. The homes of athletes have trophies on the shelves. Hummel collectors love to display their love of fine porcelain. Movie buffs will have pictures and other memorabilia. Sports card collectors will evidence their prizes.

There is something about humans that causes us to share. What good is a victory, or a hobby, unless it can be displayed, commented on, relived, reloved?

If Jesus Christ means anything to those who believe, then sooner or later he will find ways to show up in our lives, homes and conversations. People will notice books on our desk or a picture on our wall. Time will be used differently; words will be chosen with greater care and potential for love.

As disciples get better at ordering their lives according to Jesus' priorities, then there is even a point where it is difficult to determine where Jesus ends and we begin. Like the consummate bowler, or fantastic fan, a peaceful demeanor and love-motivated lifestyle begin to carry themselves beyond the church walls. We become walking advertisements for Jesus!

Ephesians 2:8-9 says, "For it is by grace you have been saved, through faith—and this not from yourselves, it is the gift of God—not by works, so that no one can boast." This means that we have a gift, eternal life, given solely by the good will of God (*grace* means "undeserved favor"). That gift is worth exploring and, once we understand its value, sharing.

In this study, we will see how Jesus offered himself to a lonely Samaritan woman in need of a genuine, caring human touch. We will then discuss ways that we, too, can share the love of God with others.

Discussion

1. Describe a time when you were hurting and someone reached out to you. Describe a time when you helped a person in need.

2. When it comes to sharing your faith, are you ready, willing and able, or nervous and afraid, or somewhere in between? Explain your response.

3. What do you think are the greatest hang-ups to sharing one's faith?

4. Read John 4:4-26. Summarize the events in this passage.

5. What does verse 9 reveal about how Jews and Samaritans related?

6. What do we know about the woman's marital status (vv. 17-19)?

7. What was the woman's worship style (vv. 19-22)?

8. As she faced Jesus at the well, the woman had spiritual and emotional needs that Jesus was able to discern. What were they?

9. Although Jesus initially asked her for water, he obviously felt that he had something to offer her, not vice versa. How would you describe his approach to this woman? What do you think motivated him?

10. In verses 10 and 13-14, Jesus likens himself to living water. What did he mean by "whoever drinks the water I give him will never

thirst" and "a spring of water welling up to eternal life" (v. 14)?

11. Read John 4:27-38. In verse 35 Jesus says that the fields are ripe for harvest; that is, many people needed Jesus and were ready to hear. Do you think that is true today? Explain why or why not.

12. Who is someone you know who needs Jesus?

13. As a group, you will be sharing Jesus with one another and growing in your faith. You will also need to share your faith, as Jesus did, so that others may meet Christ in their own way. Discuss each of the following ways to share, and see if there are any you may choose to adopt now, later, or both.

- *Idea 1:* Include an empty chair at your meetings and pray at each meeting for the person who is to sit in the chair.

- *Idea 2:* Have each group member makes a list of friends, family and neighbors who live in the area. Begin praying for at least one person (individually or as a group) and, ultimately, begin inviting these individuals to a meeting.

- *Idea 3:* Maintain an open group. This means that the group welcomes new members. During times of intense spiritual growth, you may close for a period.

- *Idea 4:* Perhaps one month out of every year, reconstitute yourself as an evangelistic small group, inviting friends and preparing to meet the Jesus of the Gospels.

- Pray together, remembering requests from previous weeks and naming before God some of the individuals you want to know Jesus.

TRAINING RESOURCES

PART I: HOW TO TRAIN SMALL GROUP LEADERS

This special section has been created with the coordinator of small group leader training in mind. You and your church will probably receive the most benefit if you can work with a committee (perhaps your Christian education committee) or the pastoral staff of your church to answer some important questions.

LAYING THE GROUNDWORK

Although many churches using this book will already have a small group ministry in place, not all will have considered the basic issues that better ensure the success of a healthy ministry. Others may be starting up new ministries. To facilitate the process of organizing a healthy ministry, here are seven questions to prayerfully consider:

1. What is the vision for small groups at our church? This question is fundamental. Answering it requires asking two more questions. First, what is our overall vision for what small groups can and will do in our church? (And, if possible, ask, What is our biblical basis?) Second, what are some of the different kinds of people in our church who can and must be touched by the small group ministry?

2. What kinds of groups will we utilize, and what characteristics will they each possess? Once you have a clear understanding of the first question, you can then plan to implement the kinds of groups that you will choose to use. Chapter four includes a number of assumptions and questions about the specific components of a healthy group and offers various group options.

3. How will we "fill" these groups with people? This question is basic to the success of small group ministry, because in the final analysis, people will only go to the kind of group that best meets (and continues to meet) their needs. Consider how to recruit the people whose needs these groups will meet.

4. Who will lead these groups? There is much more to training than taking people through a course or book like this one. For instance, consider whether you will have a program of "apprenticing," where leaders-in-training get hands-on training.

5. How will we ensure the growth of this ministry? Unless growth occurs, stagnation and eventual death often follow. Wisely plan for the continued growth of the ministry. What goals do we have for six months? one year? five years? How will we deal with a group once it has twelve members (or, how can we help groups to effect positive group births)? How will we continue to recruit members and leaders for this ministry?

6. What kind of accountability will we require of leaders? Few people function at maximum effectiveness when left to their own devices. What kind of ongoing training will we provide our leaders? What kinds of reporting will we require, and how often? What about periodic meetings? Who will oversee the ministry in general?

7. How can we communicate our unique ministry desires with potential leaders and members? Many churches with dynamic small group ministries will sit down with their answers to the above questions and "codify" them into a small group manual or a philosophy statement. This will help the ministry leaders to communicate their particular vision and mode of operation to those who will choose to participate. When structuring the min-

istry statement, you may develop it in three sections. The first section can include the vision and biblical basis for groups. The second can present the idea of leadership and accountability. The third can present the framework, resources and types of groups.

USING THIS BOOK

Your church's small group philosophy will provide a framework for thinking about the small group ministry in your church, but this manual can be the backbone for small group leader training. Here are a number of ways that you can make use of this resource:

1. *Read and lead.* Some individuals may choose to pick up this book and read it through on their own. Although this course will be most effective in a group atmosphere, individuals can learn from their own motivated study.

2. *Apprenticing.* Basically, apprenticing involves allowing a leader-in-training to learn at a slightly slower and potentially more effective pace while practicing various aspects of ministry. Some churches will require apprentice leaders to be involved in a small group for a specified period of time under the direct supervision of a small group leader. Then, apprentices can take the course and move out on their own.

3. *Four plus eight.* This book was designed so that leaders-in-training do not necessarily have to attend a full twelve-week course. Instead, the first four chapters contain all of the basic information necessary to begin leading a small group. These four chapters can be covered in a weekend or in a month. Then you can continue with the rest of the chapters on a more leisurely basis, perhaps monthly.

4. *Twelve-week intensive course.* Some coordinators will choose to take groups of leaders-in-training through a full twelve-week course. Making use of the questions, chapters and exercises, and adding in

your own church's strategy and resource materials, you can create a one-hour-per-week course, or a one-and-a-half hour course, or even a two-hour course.

LEADING THIS COURSE

Once you have answered the basic questions found in the two sections above, here are a few items related to preparation.

Time and place. Look for comfort, quiet, enough room, possible access to refreshments, a location convenient to all, and a room layout conducive to learning.

Preparation. The coordinator does not need to be any more an expert on small groups than the average member. But you must be better prepared. If you come into a meeting with a scattered and disjointed manner, then your effectiveness will be greatly limited. Put the maximum amount of time that you can into this course, realizing that the dividends will come later.

Laying out the course. You will see from this book and its appendices that there are several different elements available for the learning event.

- Questions for review that can be used to reinforce the teaching, located at the end of each chapter

- Small group exercises to enhance the lessons, found at the end of each chapter

- Your own church's strategy and resource guides or materials

APPENDIX C
RESOURCES FOR BUILDING STRONG GROUPS

The resources in appendix C are meant to guide small group coordinators or committees in creating and implementing a small group strategy. For a more detailed resource, see Jeff Arnold, *Starting Small Groups* (Abingdon Press).

1. To get people in groups:

- Include six weeks of small group participation in all new-member courses.

- Use publicity brochures and newsletter articles to encourage people to join.

- Small group leaders and groups can recruit for their own groups.

2. To help people grow, have available:

- Well-trained leaders who are ready to help people "get on track" with Christ.

- Different kinds of groups tailored to the needs of your church or fellowship.

- The challenge for discipleship offered with each kind of group.

- Differing levels of leadership within the group.

3. To help the small group grow:

- Use Serendipity's *empty chair* (put out a chair each week which represents people you would like to have in your group) so that the group is always praying for others.

- Share with other leaders a vision for spiritual growth and outreach.
- Evolve toward a mission emphasis with time.
- Recognize that some groups will become evangelistic groups.
- Encourage all members to bring friends.

4. **To develop the "mother group" idea:**

- As groups grow, they can be broken into smaller units of four for study and prayer.
- Apprentices will complete leader training and begin their own groups, possibly "daughter groups" from the "mother" group.
- Other groups continue to grow and "birth" new daughter groups.
- Daughter groups will grow to become mother groups.

5. **To ensure a strong leadership foundation:**

- *Level 1.* There will be a constant search for apprentice leaders.
- *Level 2.* Apprentice leaders will be trained to become small group leaders.
- *Level 3.* Small group leaders who have overseen "daughtering" will become coordinators or coaches.

DEVELOPING A HANDBOOK FOR YOUR PROGRAM

In appendix B, I discussed the questions a small group coordinator must ask when laying out the essentials of a small group ministry. The following is an outline of a sample manual with a statement of the vision for small group ministry to help you create your own program.

CONTENTS

Sample outline of a small group ministry manual

SMALL GROUP LEADERSHIP STRATEGY

1. *The Big Book on Small Groups* is used to train initial leaders in a four-week course, with monthly training thereafter.

2. The new leaders recruit their own groups.

3. As the groups mature, certain people from within will demonstrate the kinds of leadership that will make them effective small group leaders. The small group leaders will "apprentice" these people and will, over time, begin to give them greater responsibility as a way of testing their gifts.

4. When the apprentice leader is comfortable, the small group leader will take him or her through the church's small group leader's manual, making sure that the apprentice understands the vision, rationale and process for building a small group ministry.

5. The apprentice leader takes the training course based on *The Big Book on Small Groups*, and the cycle begins to repeat itself.

SMALL GROUP LEADER JOB DESCRIPTION

Character Qualities
- Maturity and consistency in leadership and growth
- Respect from members of the small group
- Growing relationship with God
- Love for others and ability to listen
- Ability to administrate and delegate responsibility
- Humility

Job Description
- Commit to leadership for one year (renewable)

- Administrate all aspects of a group's life
- Enable the group to build community
- Lead the small group according to its own covenant
- Lead the group toward outreach and evangelistic emphases over time
- Recruit people for the small group
- Pray daily for yourself, your church and the small group members
- Complete and turn in a monthly small group report
- Participate in monthly small group leader meetings

APPRENTICE LEADER JOB DESCRIPTION

Character Qualities

- Maturity and consistency in small group participation
- Respect from peers in small group ministry
- Growing relationship with God
- Love for others, ability to listen

Job Description

- Continue to grow in relation to God, self and others
- Listen with humility, receive feedback, learn, and grow
- Read the church or fellowship's small group handbook and be able to share its vision
- Take the small group leader training course and make a commitment to follow-up meetings
- Pray daily for yourself, your church and the small group members

SMALL GROUP COACH/COORDINATOR JOB DESCRIPTION

Character Qualities

- Maturity and consistent participation in small group ministry for an extended time

- Wisdom, the ability to listen and offer good counsel

- Growing relationship with God

- Lifestyle consistent with Christian values

- Gift of administration

- Discipline, a self-starter personality

- Experience with leading small groups, an understanding of the pitfalls and joys

- Experience with "mothering" a number of small groups

Job Description

- Help leaders recruit for their groups

- Instill a vision for small group ministry in the small group leaders

- Keep the pastor and other church leaders well informed

- Encourage the formation of various kinds of groups and outreach ministries

- Pray without ceasing

- Act as a pastor and support system for small group leaders

- Help small group leaders train apprentice leaders

- Develop long-term goals

SMALL GROUP LEADER'S MONTHLY REPORT
AND EVALUATION

Leader's Name _____

Date _____

Number of Meetings This Month _____

Day and Time of Group _____

Location _____

Type of Group _____

How (from 1-5, with 1 being "bad" and 5 being "terrific") do you feel about the group?

What percentage of group time do you use for

- *group building*

- *growth in relationship with God (study, worship, prayer)*

- *outreach (evangelism and mission)*

- *other*

What kinds of issues is your group working through?

What worries you about the group?

What brings you joy about the group?

In what ways is your group growing

- *in love for each other*

- *in love for God*

- *in desire for and implementation of outreach*

LEADER'S SELF-EVALUATION

React as honestly as you can to the following self-evaluation. For each character quality you will circle a number, from 1-5, based on your perception of yourself, 1 being "weak" and 5 being "strong."

A. *Relationship with God*

Desire for God's will 1 2 3 4 5

Willingness to let God have control 1 2 3 4 5

Humility 1 2 3 4 5

B. *Relationship with Self*

Self-confident 1 2 3 4 5

Aware of strengths and weaknesses 1 2 3 4 5

Risk-taking 1 2 3 4 5

Ethical 1 2 3 4 5

C. *Relationship with Others*

Nurturing 1 2 3 4 5

Sensitive in listening 1 2 3 4 5

Vulnerable 1 2 3 4 5

Serving 1 2 3 4 5

Willing to give leadership away 1 2 3 4 5

Time and energy 1 2 3 4 5

Now that you have completed the chart, show it to a friend whom you trust and who can be honest with you. Discuss each characteristic and allow him or her to help you shape your perceptions. Once you have done this, you will know the areas in which you should grow.

SMALL GROUP EVALUATION

When evaluating, it is helpful to answer the following questions:

1. Effectiveness of group at making disciples. *Where is the group or each individual compared to*

- *one month ago*

- *six months ago*

- *one year ago*

2. Group status. *How we are doing as a group with*

- *group relationships*

- *group or individual strengths*

- *group or individual weaknesses*

- *effectiveness of the program (study, prayer, worship and so on)*

- *leadership development*

- *growth in discipleship*

3. Group objectives. *As a group, we need to work on*

- ☐ *correcting weaknesses (from above)*

- ☐ *enhancing strengths (from above)*

- ☐ *trying new ideas*

4. Program ideas. *To work on our objectives, we want to try ideas that*

- ☐ *correct weaknesses*

- ☐ *enhance strengths*

- ☐ *take us in new directions*

Scripture Index